Francis Allan Chapman

TALKING TO THE WORLD
FROM PAN AM'S
CLIPPERS

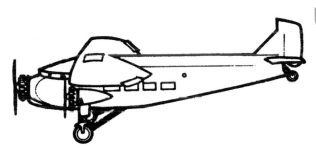

ISBN 911868-91-7

Copyright @ 1999 by Francis Allan Chapman

Send stamped addressed envelope for current book catalog.

Carstens
PUBLICATIONS, INC.
P. O. Box 700, Newton, New Jersey 07860

Author Francis Allan Chapman, FRO.
Photo PAA, Pan Am Historical Foundation

High Flight

Oh, I have slipped the surly bonds of earth
    And danced the skies on laughter-silvered wings.
Sunward I've climbed, and joined the tumbling mirth
    Of sun-split clouds—and done a hundred things.
You have not dreamed of—wheeled and soared and swung,
    High in the sunlit silence. Hov'ring there,
I've chased the shouting wind along, and flung
    My eager craft through footless halls of air.
Up, up, the long, delirious, burning blue
    I've topped the windswept heights with easy grace.
Where never a lark, or even an eagle flew
    And, whilst with silent, lifting mind I've trod
The high untrespassed sanctity of space,
    Put out my hand, and touched the face of GOD.

**John Gillespie Magee Jr
(1922-1941)**

Introduction

This memoir I am writing about concerns real life memories of my worldwide flying adventures aboard Pan American Airways Clippers as a Flight Radio Officer from 1939 to 1949. This was when President Juan Trippe was expanding his airline into Central and South America and even the rest of the world. The arrival of World War II helped PAA's explosive expansion and his company quickly became known as America's "Chosen Instrument". Trippe's ambition and vision along with his international diplomacy and intrigue plus his financial manipulations helped make Pan Am the worlds largest and greatest International airline.

Millions of memories have I, that float around in my head. But at times a simple fact that I really know well, will drift away like a cloud in a breeze. So when this happens, when fact slips into fiction, please forgive this lapse, the story must go on.

This memoir is written in 1994, as a chronological diary, but covers my memories of 1939-1949. I've described the very rapid technological advance in radio equipment and improved performance of 14 different aircraft Clippers from the Sikorsky S-38 twin engined 8 passenger seaplane that flew at 105 MPH, through to the Boeing B-377 Stratocruiser four engined 86 passenger landplane that flew at 275 MPH.

I've written this for my children; Allan, Kenneth, Jeanne and Connie as well as for my wife Jean and the rest of my extended family. But also it's for my old Pan American friends and to all aviation history buffs.

There are two stars in this memoir, my beautiful former wife Florence Ann Rodgers Chapman and Pan American Airways. (PAA) I've tried to tell you how I felt way back when. There were a jillion or more loving times I enjoyed with Florence Ann, in my Pan American Airways days. She was my inspiration and I dedicate this memoir to her.

Blended along with those lovely memories are a hundred or two thrilling flights with PAA, that took me into another dimension. The MAGIC MOMENT of takeoff on each flight was some kind of an ethereal experience for me that continues to this day. I hope the reader gets a touch of those early sensations that I'll try hard to faithfully describe. I did the background research on my story at the University of Massachusetts library. Robert Daley's book titled "An American Saga - Juan Trippe and his Pan Am Empire" filled my needs the best. Daley extensively characterized Pan Am's President Juan Trippe along with Andre Priester and Hugo Leuteritz. I've quoted a few excerpts about the Communications and Navigations equipment Radio Engineering Expert Hugo Leuteritz developed for PAA.

Hopefully, his experiences will show why dependable two way radio and Navigational direction finding (DF) equipment was a must on all over-ocean flights and should be operated by professional Flight Radio Officers (FRO) This would provide the proper elements to help assure safer flights in case of any emergencies or adverse weather conditions that might arise.

One of my writing goals is to show the Flight Radio Officers' point of view, in relation to the rest of the smoothly operating flight cockpit crew. Our essential tasks were to provide good in-flight two way communication with ground control radio stations giving aircraft progress reports, direction finding aids and weather. I have quoted from President Trippe's 1941 Royal Academy "Ocean Air Transport" speech in London that illustrated this well.

"The Flight Radio Officer is responsible for the operation of the plane's complete radio equipment and for maintenance of constant communication with the radio control stations ashore. On duty he is a rather busy airman. At a minimum, he must contact his watch ground station every fifteen minutes. On the half hour and on the hour he must transmit the ship's position and on hour, in addition to the position, a complete report on its navigation and progress, the track made good, winds, weather and general conditions. He constantly receives weather reports, bearings from ground stations and in turn himself taking radio bearings upon surface stations or upon any available ships within range."

"Radio equipment carried by a Clipper consists of two completely interchangeable telegraph and telephone transmitters, which can operate on either high or low frequency, thereby providing for communication with surface vessels as well as the ground control stations. The ship also has two receivers, the function of which are interchangeable, and which cover frequency bands of 200 to 18,000 kcs. There is also an automatic direction finder which can be manually operated. An additional receiver for radio telephone operation, controllable from the pilots' seat, is carried for use within 60 miles of the terminal stations, in conjunction with the regular transmitters. For ground to air and point to point communications, the ground control stations are equipped with from three to five transmitters, of various power outputs, together with the necessary receiving equipment. Each station, in addition, is usually equipped with radio navigation facilities. Normal communication ranges are in the neighborhood of 3,600 miles."

TOP OPPOSITE: Pan American Airways System company photo taken when author Francis Allan Chapman, 23, was hired as Flight Radio Officer May 1939. Note uniform cap emblem of North and South American continents with initials PAA. PAA, Pan Am Historical Foundation

COVER: Pan Am's Sikorsky S-42 BRAZILIAN CLIPPER arriving at Rio de Janeiro to be christened, August 18, 1934. This painting is one of a series published by Pan Am in 1963 by artist John T. McCoy. Pan American World Airways. Collection of Arthur Prado.

Acknowledgments

I want to thank and acknowledge help and contributing stories, photos, charts and other data I've received from a few old friends. We flew together as Pan American Airways Flight Radio Officers, 1939-1949. They include: Orville Bivens, Charles Chase, Ralph Conly, Charles Liese, Carl Sammy Mason, Fred Mathews, Arthur Prado, Harold Richardson, Don Thomas, William Todd, George Whitaker and John Willmott. Thanks go to my special friends Barbara Blodgett, Justin Hartman, Don Herr and Ray Wyman for providing listening ears and helped me keep my goals straight.

More special thanks go to Ralph Conly who is the FRO's unofficial historian, video taper of the 50th reunion of FROs and the keeper upper of all our many address changes through his Pan-Am Communications Old Timers list. Still more thanks goes to Bill Todd who recently mailed me some very special old stuff such as a copy of the Nov. 1941 "New Horizons" magazine, old PAA baggage stickers, and 50 photos of young kids who used to be FROs 55 years ago. Publisher Hal Carstens has added later PAA jet aircraft from his personal collection used by Pan Am until it ceased operation.

Obvious and deep felt appreciation and thanks go to my dear loving wife Jean Russ Chapman, who is a retired children's book editor. Her understanding, patience and noninterference with my story is understood and welcomed. The story is all mine, sentence structure, dangling participles, redundancies, pontifications and all.

I have quoted from Robert Daley's book titled "An American Saga-Juan Trippe and His Pan American Empire" as well as from "Pictorial History of Pan American World Airways" by P. St. John Turner and "Pan American's Ocean Clippers" by Barry Taylor.

Pan American Airways (PAA), Pan American World Airways, Pan Am, and the Company, will be used interchangeably throughout my story. I am indebted to the many persons and organizations who have provided photographs and art for this book and we have credited these under the illustration wherever possible. Readers should note that the Pan American World Airways photo and art collection is now shared by the Pan Am Historical Foundation in New York City and the University of Miami, Richter Library Archives and Special Collections.

Pan American's first passenger flight from Key West, Florida, to Havana, Cuba, took place on January 16, 1928, using a Fokker F-7 triplane. Commercial aviation was in its infancy. Air terminals were spartan, lacking almost all amenities. Pan American World Airways painting by John T. McCoy

Contents

Juan T. Trippe

Pan American Historical Foundation

This painting is of Juan T, Trippe, President and Chief Executive Officer of Pan American World Airways-Pan Am, the worlds most experienced airline. Mr. Trippe had energetic drive, was a financier, quiet, serious, imaginative, and with perseverance. He was a goal oriented young man who learned his fine negotiating skill from debating at Yale. He built the greatest airline in the world which he ran successfuly for over 50 years.

Trippe was born June 27, 1899 into a banking family. At 17 he went to Marconi Radio School to learn radio theory and Morse code. Then he attended the private Curtiss Flying School. At 18 he enrolled at Yale. But at the end of his freshman year he left to join the Marine Corp in 1917. Because there was no pilot training there, he got himself transferred to the Navy. He was sent to Massachusetts Institute of Technology for ground school and soloed in a Jenny, later a seaplane at Hampton Roads, Va. His main goals were radio and flying.

On his discharge from the Navy, he returned to Yale, taking business courses. He was on the football, rowing and golfing teams until a football injury prevented him from continuing those very physically active sports until much later. He formed the Yale Flying Club and bought a Jenny. Because of his especially fine knowledge of flight mechanics he reworked the incident of the dihedral to increase his planes speed. He won a race over Long Island against ten other planes by six seconds. When Trippe graduated from Yale at 23, he had decided he wanted to make a business out of aviation. His piloting dare devil attitude didn't fit his basic shy personality. But he had the right qualifications to succeed in developing an airline.

He wanted to buy planes. Using his father's inheritance, and money from his Yale classmates like Whitney, Vanderbilt and across the street neighbor William Rockefeller, he was able to purchase seven war surplus planes.

After he and his pilot friends assembled the planes he formed his first airline, Long Island Airways. Later he designed and modified the planes to carry two passengers. No one else had done this in 1922. He was only 23 and had just doubled his planes carrying capacity and his income soared. He realized then that it would be possible for aircraft to be made bigger and fly faster and over greater distances. He felt he had the secret formula. He went on from his seven pilot and seven plane Long Island Airways, to continue his explosive expansion into an airline of the world. In the process he founded Alaskan Air Transport, Buffalo Airlines, Eastern Air Transport, Colonial Air Transport and merged or bought out many others until his formation of Pan American World Airways of Key West, FL with his first airmail flight between Key West and Havana, Cuba on Aug. 15, 1927. Trippe was a rare twentieth century aviation visionary. Aviation history will long remember his many accomplishments and contributions to world aviation.

Chapter 1
First Stop Havana

ime flies when you are having fun. And I was certainly enjoying myself with all that I was learning and the exotic foreign countries I was about to visit.

I must have been making good progress in my Pan American Airways training because it seemed only a short time after I was hired, that the exciting moment arrived when I found my name posted for my first flight. The flight schedule board at the radio station was inside the Pan American Airways International terminal at Dinner Key, in Miami. This board was always a hub of activities, as it was where all the flight crews could find out when and where they were going next. It showed plane number, pilots name, route, time of departure. NC80V, Pilot Capt. Doxey, Miami-Havana, FRO Chapman, 7/22 Depart 0800. Man was that an exciting moment in my young life when I saw my name listed. Date, July 22, 1939.

The morning of my first flight I probably awoke at 5 AM.

ABOVE: This modest sidewalk operations office in Key West, Florida is the birthplace of Pan American Airways System. The airline's first scheduled international air mail flight took off from Key West bound for Havana, Cuba, a distance of 90 miles. The Fokker F7 NC53, trimotor land plane the *General Machado* that left with many bags of mail on Oct. 28, 1927. Pan Am Historical Foundation

BELOW: Three young and bold roommates hired as PAA Flight Radio Officers, left to right, Oscar Olsen, the author and Charles Chase. Sikorsky S-40 seaplane NC80V in rear would carry Chapman on his first international flight to Havana, July 22, 1939. Frank Chapman

I rushed through breakfast, got into my brand new Flight Radio Officer uniform, shined my shoes again and ran to the radio station to pick up the log sheets and DF charts only to find out the ground crew hadn't finished with their own pre-flight checks. So I'm sure I was pacing around the terminal muttering to myself. Just had to wait for the beaching crew to get NC80V into the water. I must have finished my preflight check at least an hour before departure It included running all the equipment and making a quick CW code check with the radioman on the aircraft flight watch at WKDL, The Communications Center for the airline. I would be talking with him half way to Havana and back, every 15 minutes while we were in flight. Each crew member had to do his own preflight checkout well before departure time and then return to the terminal to wait.

The Captain and copilot were doing their thing in the operations office getting the latest weather, winds aloft and souls on board (SOB). Their major concern was to carefully check the weight and balance of the plane before takeoff. This included getting the correct weight of the fuel plus enough gas to reach an alternate landing area in case the destination weather had deteriorated, making a last minute diversion necessary. Any crew member in charge of loading fuel unofficially added about 50 extra gallons of gas as "pocket gas" or "gas for Mama" if he was married. This would give a small margin of safety in case winds were stronger than forecast. The weight and balance load figures were critical and had to be accurate, otherwise the center of gravity (CG), would be off and the plane would have trouble lifting off the water. All skippers knew about pocket gas and automatically figured in the extra

ABOVE: Pan American Airways System international seaplane terminal at Dinner Key, Coconut Grove, Florida. Two Sikorsky S-42 seaplanes are seen in foreground with hangars in background. Top right is U. S. Coast Guard Station. BELOW: Another view of the Dinner Key Terminal with hundreds of weekend tourists and guests watching the exciting arrivals and departures of PAA planes to such exotic cities as Buenos Aires, San Juan, Panama, Havana, Kingston and Rio de Janeiro. Pan American World Airways

330 lbs weight.

The moment of departure had arrived, I was 23 years old and I was ready and excited. Impatiently I waited for the skipper to give us the word, march. At last he did. So we tried to stay in step while we shuffled on board the S-40 Sikorsky NC80V, followed by 30 passengers. The two stewards got every one settled and seat belted, while the Skipper and copilot went through their takeoff check list. Altimeter set, read fuel gauges, master power switch on, ignition switches on, and advance throttles. I had nothing to do but watch.

Finally all four engines were started, the docking lines were dropped and we slowly moved away from the dock. The copilot called the Panair I launch to see if our take-off area was clear and began taxiing out into Biscayne Bay.

I know I must have been on cloud 9, I was so keyed up. We swung into the wind. Capt. Doxey checked with Panair I once more and found the takeoff area was still clear. He pushed the throttles slowly forward and we picked up speed quickly. Within ten seconds the plane tipped forward slightly, onto the step. We were now skimming along over the calm Bay at 50 MPH. This is when the captain gently pulled back on the steering column and we lifted off the water. Wow! We were flying!! This was the most thrilling time for me that I'd ever had in my life. Everything began to miniaturize: the bay, people at the terminal, nearby sailboats, all speedily grew tiny. It was a very special moment for me. I felt this was an ethereal sensation rather hard to describe. But I have felt this with almost every takeoff throughout my life. It all began on Biscayne Bay at Dinner Key, Miami, Fl. that sunny morning in July.

Charles and Anne Lindbergh and Betty and Juan Trippe beside a Sikorsky S-38, during the first airmail flight between the United States and South America in September 1929, cutting weeks off the delivery of letters. PAA, Univ. of Miami, Richter Library

The skipper continued a slow banking climb to the southwest until we reached 1,000 feet. He leveled off at this altitude. I was peering intensely out the cockpit window. All I could see was sunny skies and the blue green Gulf stream visible below. Stretching all around us and far beyond was the Caribbean. 220 miles away was our destination. Cruising at 115 MPH, we'd be there in two hours.

Except for three or four brief radio contacts my radio was quiet. However I was kept busy taking radio bearings from all directions. I wanted to practice my new skills.

I kept handing a steady flow of little slips of paper to the skipper. They had broadcast station call letters, the time and a number representing the bearing from plane to the station. CMA 355 meant a Havana station was 5 degrees off our port bow. Or WKEY 045 meant a Key West station was 45 degrees off our starboard bow. I could estimate how far away from Key West we were when we passed by. If it took us 12 minutes for the bearing to change from 045 to 090, than I would multiply 12 times 2 or 24 miles. That indicated that we were 24 miles off Key West. The number 2 was a constant, representing the plane's air speed over the water of 2 miles per minute.

Time sped by. All too quickly I was peering over the copi-

Top: PAA President Juan Trippe with Col. Charles Lindberg, Pan American's Technical Director, in front of Fokker F10 prior to takeoff on the first airmail flight to San Juan, Puerto Rico. This event coincided with the opening of the new PAA international seaplane terminal at Dinner Key, 1929. PAA, University of Miami, Richter Library (ASC)

BELOW: Another photo of Sikorsky S-38 NC146M, the fourteenth S-38 delivered to Pan American Airways, in Miami, Oct. 16, 1929. Frank Chapman

Earl "Pappy" Martin, Flight Radio Officer instructor and FRO Horatio "Rebel" Frazer was in his white overalls waiting for the Panair launch to take them into Biscayne Bay for more hours of radio direction finder training. This was part of the two to three month training each FRO received before being assigned to flight duty . William Todd

Pappy Martin headed out into the Bay with FROs for their DF practice. It was an important essential for the FROs to learn DF procedures thoroughly. The radio DF procedure was the only system available at that time that could assist the captain in making a successful instrument landing in bad weather in that early stage of aviation expansion into Central and South America. William Todd

lot's shoulder again scanning the horizon ahead. Havana Bay whose name I can't recall at the moment, began magically to grow larger and more distinct. Soon we started our descent. Had to hurry back and reel in my 150 feet of trailing antenna. I didn't want to forget that before we landed in the bay. Bad news for me if I did. We got clearance to land from the Panair boat that had cleared the landing area. Doxey "greased one on" meaning he'd made an ultra smooth landing. We slowly taxied toward the dock while the copilot opened the bow hatch so he

could reach out and pick up the docking lines. It had taken us 2:05 minutes from Miami to Havana. I was so happy to have done my bit toward making the flight safe and easy, with no problems. My return flight to Miami, in the late afternoon was uneventful, arriving at 5:10 PM. Thus ended my very first roundtrip passenger flight to a foreign country.

PAA bought fourteen Consolidated Commodore flying boats from New York - Buenos Aires Airlines in 1930. This fleet of flying boats helped complete the air link from Miami down the east coast of South America to Buenos Aires, another step in President Juan Trippe's airline expansion plans. Carrying 29 passengers the ship had a 102 mph cruising speed. Several of the Commodores were used for crew member training when Chapman joined the company in 1939. Pan American Airways photo.

Earlier, when in regular service, the Commodore seated 29 passengers with a comfortable lounge area. The leg room was greater than in today's jumbo jets. Arthur Prado

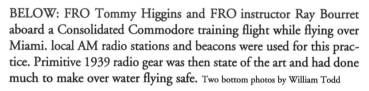

Mystery twin engined cockpit photo which the author believes was the early Consolidated Commodore. Notice the simplicity of the dashboard especially when compared to modern jets. William Todd

BELOW: FRO Tommy Higgins and FRO instructor Ray Bourret aboard a Consolidated Commodore training flight while flying over Miami. local AM radio stations and beacons were used for this practice. Primitive 1939 radio gear was then state of the art and had done much to make over water flying safe. Two bottom photos by William Todd

LOWER RIGHT: Henry Nicks and Pete Petrogalas, two of the PAA flight control radio station operators at WKDL, located in the Dinner Key passenger terminal. The station was in contact with PAA radio stations in over 20 countries in the Carribean, Central and South America, as well as with FRO's on outgoing and incoming flights.

Chapter 2
A Young Man Named Francis Goes to Radio School

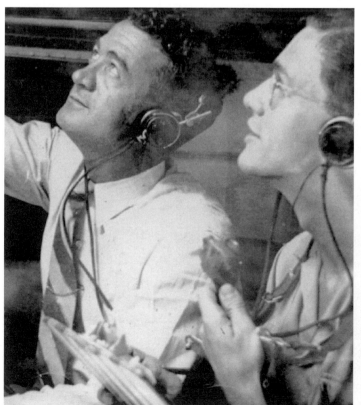

What's the sky like Dad? Why is it blue? There are "way back when" memories of a little guy named Francis, who flew his Grandpa Brewer's home made kites in a field of new mown hay at York Beach, Maine.

Later I recall when I graduated from climbing tall oaks for fun. Five or six of my high school gang dared each other to climb the Salmon Falls, N. H. water tower at midnight. We were sitting on the circular walkway 100 feet in the air, when a night watchman with a flashlight yelled for us to get down now! I think he swore at us. We quietly shivered atop the tower hoping he'd finally go away. Which of course he did. My

UPPER LEFT: FRO Charlie Chase at WKDL training as a station operator. Charlie flew for a while but later the company transferred him to Port au Prince as station HHP radio operator. Ralph Conly

UPPER RIGHT: FRO Oscar Olsen ready to leave on a Sikorsky S-42 for San Juan. By 1939 PAA was flying to China, Australia, New Zealand, Alaska, Central and South America, Cuba, and other Carribbean points. Frank Chapman

BELOW: Author's second flight to Havana was on this Sikorsky S-40, NC752V. Note the crowd of tourists and well wishers on open terminal balcony. William Todd

UPPER LEFT: Florence Ann Rodgers at the Cabana Beach Club, Miami Beach, Florida, then an employee at the Pan American radio station WKDL at Dinner Key. Francis Chapman

UPPER RIGHT: Mr. and Mrs. Francis Chapman honeymooning at grandpa Luther Brewer's York Beach, Maine, summer cottage, May 19, 1940. Europe was already at war. Francis Chapman

BELOW: The S-40 docked in Havana was the one Chapman flew aboard on his first flight to Havana. Docked behind the S-40 is a passenger ship that took about 24 hours to sail from Miami to Havana. The Pan American S-40 made the trip in 2 hours, 8 minutes. Francis Chapman

adventures were getting a little bolder.

From the time I was 12 until I left for the sea at 20, our family that included Mom-Florence, Dad-Fred, brother Paul and me. We lived with my mother's parents Vida and Luther Brewer. Grandma was sick for years, Mom took care of her. My Grandpa called Gramp was my role model. His skills and interests were similar to mine. First he was a religious man. He tutored me in carpentry, electricity and fix-it tasks around the house. These intrigued me. And he was available. Whereas Dad, a teacher and school principal, had lots of after school activities as well as nightly meetings. So I didn't see lots of him. Besides Dad enjoyed arts, botany, various crafts and music which didn't interest me much then. Dad and Mom both helped me with my homework, especially Mom, as she had

UPPER LEFT: FRO Carl "Sammy" Mason was still aboard the crashed S43 in Morant bay, Kingston, Jamaica. He was reporting crash details to WKDL and San Juan ground control station when Capt. Hart shouted to get the H off before the plane sank. Captain Hart and copilot Allen are ready to jump into a life raft. All passengers and crew were saved by Steamer SS Cavina. Carl Mason

UPPER RIGHT: A Sikorsky S42 N 15376 Clipper Dominican crashed in San Juan harbor October 3, 1941. Fuselage was being recovered but have no other details. PAA, Pan Am Historical Foundation

LOWER LEFT: Hugo Leuteritz of RCA, who Juan Trippe hired as a consultant to develop aircraft Direction Finding (DF) and communications equipment for PAA. He designed the loop antenna attached to a receiver that indicated what direction radio beacon and radio broadcast signals were coming from. University of Miami, Richter Library

LOWER RIGHT: Leuteritz's prototype design of the DF loop (square wooden frame, top left) Pilots felt was too flimsy to trust its use, circa 1928. Later, it was proven to be essential for a good basic navigational aid for over-water flights until more sophisticated equipment was designed. Pan Am Historical Foundation

ABOVE: The S-38 carried eight passengers at 105 MPH, fast fot its day, with a range of 300 miles. It had a two man crew, the FRO sat in the right seat. This is a sister plane flown by the author to Merida. Note that no flight instruments visible. FRO sent his CW radio messages with the code key clipped to his knee.He also served the famous PAA cold chicken box lunches to passengers. After landing, he picked up the buoy line when Skipper got close enough to reach. Pan Am Historical. Foundation, University of Miami, Richter Library

LEFT: Early model Pan American radio regeneration receiver model ACC, serial #56. Believe the front panel hinged outward to change inductance coils to cover different aircraft frequencies. Believe it went with the PAA 10F3 transmitter with about 10/ 15 watts output. FRO Chapman believes these were the models they had to tear down and rebuild during training at Dinner Key. Ralph Conly

ABOVE: This later model S-38 had more comfortable, sturdier passenger seats than ones first delivered. Look at the large picture windows, plush seats, legroom. PAA, Pan Am Historical Foundation

RIGHT: Frank Chapman's FCC second class radio telegraph operator license, issued June 12, 1935 at Boston, Massachusetts. Francis Chapman

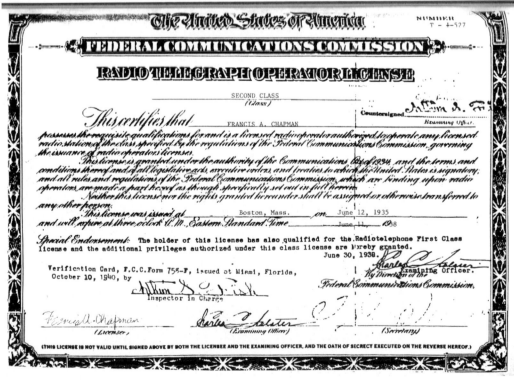

ABOVE: Aware of the mystique of overseas commercial aviation by thousands who had never flown, Pan American Airways sponsored Visitor's Days, in which the public was invited for a walk-through tour. Here a crowd of visitors await their turn to inspect this glamorous new method of ocean travel. This was a Sikorsky S-42A, NC15376 *Clipper Dominican*.

BELOW: S-42 *Clipper Brazilian* is disembarking passengers from Nassau while a steward assists passengers through the aft hatch. Ground crew stands by ready to unload baggage into baggage carts. Photos Pan Am Historical Foundation, University of Miami, Richter Library.

been an English teacher before she was married.

In my early school years, I thought I was really a dumb kid. The fact that I badly needed glasses was not discovered until I was a freshman in High School! It was incredible, what glasses did for my school work. Truly, all of a sudden I could see perfectly, no more fuzzy letters and scenery. I started doing a lot of catch up in all subjects especially reading skills. I got some A's and B's instead of the usual C's and D's. By the time I got to Massachusetts Radio School I knew I was quite intelligent.

ABOVE: Another view of Sikorsky S-42A NC822M docked while FRO Bill Todd's test hop aboard a Sikorsky S-41 taxis towards the ramp and hangar for maintenance. William Todd

BELOW: A Pan American flight returning from Merida is being pulled up the ramp for maintenance. Some of the beaching crew is a new flight crew in training. William Todd

In my mind's eye I can look back to when I was almost 15, and lying on our sunny lawn at our summer cottage at York Beach, staring into the blue. Day dreaming I guess. It was then that I heard a quiet roar that became thunderous overhead. I'd seen pictures of what quickly disappeared just beyond the nearby woods. I knew it was a plane and thought it might have crashed. But I hadn't heard any noise or didn't see smoke. I raced through the woods and saw this odd "thing" sitting in neighbor Ernst's field. It turned out to be a barn-stormer and his single engine biplane, tied together with lots of wires. I'm sure I stared wide eyed and open mouthed at the man standing beside the plane. He seemed like a god. But I found he was real, since he offered me a chance to climb into the cockpit for a minute while he waited for people to gather.

I never did get that free ride he hinted at. I helped him by holding his wing tip while he turned into the wind for take-offs. I watched him take a few passengers up for a five minute flight. Guess he didn't make much money that day. I began to dream of soaring through the air somewhere, some how, sometime. I'm sure I dreamed in technicolor that night.

In the summer of 1931, I started to work at the A and P Grocery store in York Village. And I also caddied at the York Village Country Club two summers. My savings went toward buying a bicycle.

ABOVE: The larger S-42 being towed up ramp while flight crew in training prepares to position heavy duty wheeled dolly under the center of plane. Engines still idling keep plane correctly positioned while its towed. William Todd

BELOW: The same S-42 inside hanger for maintenance work . Pan American had developed extensive and strict maintenance schedules to follow. These safety rules had been set by V. P. Andre Preister who was ultra safety conscious. It was felt essential for PAA's continued growth, to maintain a fine safety record. Frank Chapman

ABOVE LEFT: Roommates Charlie Chase and Frank Chapman in front of #2 hanger while leaning on Chapman's 1936 Dodge in their "girl chasing" outfits. Even then aircraft hangars were large.

ABOVE RIGHT: FRO Frank Chapman standing on Captain's seat in cockpit of S-40 Caribbean Clipper. Pan American's world and wings logo was emblazoned and every aircraft in the PAA fleet.

LEFT CENTER: Chapman is congratulating his roommate, Oscar Olsen. He's got a date with Minnie Lee and is borrowing Chapman's car.

LEFT BOTTOM: Ready for a swim at Matheson's Hammock Beach. Photos this page by Frank Chapman

Money was short when I graduated from Dover, N. H. High School in 1933. As an example, Dad was a grammar school principal in South Berwick, Maine and had to work during the school vacation to keep things afloat financially. We weren't poor but just making it I guess. Every summer he worked as the head waiter at the Passaconway Inn at York Cliffs.

Luckily, President Roosevelt's National Recovery Act (NRA) had just been passed. Funding for entry level jobs in most businesses around the country could be arranged through the NRA. In the fall of 1933, my next door neighbor Dr. George Nutter found he could offer me a job at his Drug Store using this plan. So I took the soda jerk's job at $10. for a 48 hour week and was able to save enough for Massachusetts Radio School tuition in Boston. Dr. Nutter drove me the three miles from home to his drug store each morning, so I could open at 7 AM. In the evening, I locked up at 6 PM and walked home the three miles every night. That started my life long practice of walking just about every day. I can tell you it seemed a long and lonely walk through the snow drifts, those winter nights. With no street lights either. I worked a year at the store and got a bad case of chocolate milk shakeitis along with ice cream frappes. Couldn't get enough of them.

The fall of 1934 I registered at Mass. Radio for the radio classes that prepared me to take the FCC telegraph and telephone licenses. My class was small, maybe 25 students. The courses were easy, mainly radio theory, with very little hands on experience. Studied fairly extensive FCC rules and regula-

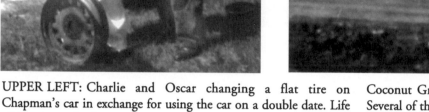

UPPER LEFT: Charlie and Oscar changing a flat tire on Chapman's car in exchange for using the car on a double date. Life of the airmen in the 1930s was a continual adventure.

UPPER RIGHT: Ma Sawyer's rooming house 3262 Elizabeth St.

Coconut Grove, almost across the street from the PAA terminal. Several of the FRO's lived there.

BELOW: This is the S-41, NC41V, a slightly different configuration from its sister S-38. Photos by Frank Chapman

tions. These rules covered all commercial and amateur radio broadcasts. Also we learned the International Morse code, called CW, as well as basic operating procedures.

When I earned my radiotelegraph license I'd be able to work aboard a ship or in a ship to shore coastal radio station where they communicated in Morse code. With the radiotelephone license I could work in any AM radio broadcast station as their chief engineer, keeping the station tuned and on the air, according to the FCC regulations.

I graduated in May 1935, and successfully passed the two commercial radio licensing exams given by the FCC as well as a third test for my general radio amateur license.

RCA had a monopoly on shipboard radio equipment and knew what ships required Radio Officers, called "Sparks". When I graduated the ONLY ship that needed a radio operator was a 100' long fishing trawler docked in Boston harbor. I went to look at it. I climbed aboard. The first thing that hit me was the strong fish smell. Next, the radio shack was cramped

An S-43 drones overhead ready to land in Biscayne Bay, situated between Miami and Key Largo to the south. From 1912 to 1935 the Florida East Coast Railroad provided freight and passenger service to Key West with ship service to Havana. Following the hurricane of 1935 the line was abandoned and subsequently rebuilt as U. S. Highway 1. William Todd

and on a steep slant. My sleeping cabin was not much bigger than a casket. On top of all these negatives I began to feel very funny. I climbed up on deck only to realize that I was about to be sea sick. And the ship was still tied to the dock! You know what my reaction was. I went home discouraged.

When I got home I found the First National Grocery store in South Berwick, Me. needed help. Since I had grocery clerk experience and knew the people well in the town, I was made the manager at $50. a week. I figured I'd keep busy while waiting for an opening in radio and delay my world travels.

Late one November night in 1936 as I was locking the store, my Mom phoned me. She said I had a telegram, my first. She read it to me. It said to report to Captain Lloyd Smith aboard the SS Ensley *City* at Baltimore. They needed a Radio Officer aboard before they could sail. I accepted the job immediately. At the time I didn't know I was a strike breaker or "scab". I knew not where it was bound but I didn't care. All I knew was my adventurous life was hopefully about to begin.

There's a long story here about reporting to the ship in Baltimore and all my many merchant marine experiences on the world's oceans, from Nov. 1936 to May 1939. But that's another story.

Chapter 3

Why Flight Radio Officers Were Needed. Captain Fatt's Crash

In the spring of 1939, my Radio School classmate, Don

ABOVE: S-43 NC16927 "on the step" in Biscayne Bay, 1939.
Photos this page Pan Am Historical Foundation

BELOW: Here is a Sikorsky S-41 amphibian ready to waddle up the Dinner Key ramp unassisted. PAA, Pan Am Historical Foundation

Smith told me that Pan American Airways was hiring Flight Radio Officers. I realized that was just the opportunity I'd been waiting for. So when the Texaco oil tanker *SS Arizona* that I was the Radio Officer on, docked at Savannah, I told the Skipper I was leaving the seasick sea. Because of my radio operating sea duty experience, I had been able to upgrade my FCC Second Class Radiotelegraph license to First Class. With this license and my First Class Radiotelephone license in hand, I could meet PAA's starting qualifications.

With a wad of money in my pocket, I grabbed the Greyhound bus that was headed for Miami. I expected to get a job interview with Pan American Airways the next day. This somewhat naive country boy couldn't possibly imagine all the things that were about to happen to him. I was trying to imag-

24

ABOVE: Three Boeing B307 land planes newly delivered to Latin American Division that sit at Miami's Dade County Airport. The first of the three was NC19903 *Clipper Flying Cloud* delivered Feb. 1940, later the NC19910 *Clipper Comet* and NC19902 *Clipper Rainbow* arrived. These drastically changed our flight schedules.

They were the first pressurized planes with an extended flight range that made it possible for more direct flights with fewer stops. They carried 33 passengers in spacious seating comfortably above the weather. William Todd

ine just what PAA would be like but I couldn't.

Before I start telling you of my experiences aboard Pan American Airways Clippers, I want to give you a brief background of the company to set the stage. It will also help explain why several hundred professional Flight Radio Officers were on board PAA's planes for only a little over twenty years. The main reason for this was the exceptionally rapid technological progress that was made in radio communications and navigational equipment which took place during the war years. This advanced gear would ultimately help replace us FROs and professional merchant marine navigators after 1949.

Here's an example of the dramatic equipment changes that took place in ten years. When I first started flying we were using low powered 10 watt code transmitters as no adequate voice transmitters were available. The manual direction finder didn't always give dependable bearings to navigate by. However, ten years later we were using multichannel 150 watt voice transmitters with signals that permitted the copilot to talk to either Europe or the U. S. from the middle of the Atlantic. We also had Loran (long range navigation) where any of the crew could get accurate position fixes in a minute or two while flying over either ocean. This was instead of taking 10 minutes for a celestial fix which required a clear shot at the stars. Those performances were impossible in 1939.

In my research, I found out that credit for the steadily improving radio and navigational gear for PAA should primarily be given to Hugo Leuteritz, the Radio Engineering specialist from RCA who was hired to work directly for Trippe.

His unusually practical designing skills were extremely helpful. He provided good solutions to various long distance radio communications and navigational problems.

Increasing strong support came from the Operations Manager, Andre Priester. If it hadn't been for Juan Trippe's full support of both these men, his dream of a world airline would

BELOW: The author's long time friend FRO Orville Bivens based in Rio with Chapman had a narrow escape in a landing at Rio. He transferred to the pilot group and later moved to Eastern Airlines and became a very successful Captain for over 30 years. William Todd

This Stratoliner B307 NC 19903 *Clipper Flying Cloud* originally left the Boeing Field on its inaugural tour of South American capitols to introduce the dramatically new model. It was part of the ultra secret plan between President Juan Trippe of PAA, the U. S. War Department and the President of Columbia, Eduardo Santos.

The Pan American Airways takeover of Columbia's SCADTA Airlines started when the *Clipper Flying Cloud* landed at Barrinquilla June 12, 1940 It later flew to Rio to Belem, non-stop in 6:30 hours.
William Todd

have faltered badly.

In my opinion this trio of men were the major driving force in the late 1920s and early 1930s, which pushed the company into a rapidly expanding world class airline. I hasten to mention that Trippe would have gotten nowhere without the very faithful and continuous backing of all his wealthy Yale buddies and other banking friends.

Technically, Charles Lindberg made a major contribution as well, as consultant, in flying many survey flights. They were to Mexico, the Caribbean, Alaska, China, and Europe via the Atlantic, South Africa and South America. His wife Anne provided invaluable data on seaplane landing areas, airports, radio beacons and communications information like station call letters and frequencies. He began consulting with PAA in 1927, shortly after his record breaking solo flight to Paris.

Soon after Pan American Airways made its inaugural mail flight from Key West to Havana in 1927, it began to be clear to President Juan Trippe, Andre Priester, and especially Hugo Leuteritz, that it would be necessary for the company to install dependable communications and navigation equipment aboard planes flying over water and out of sight of land. And to be operated by radio specialists. By having this equipment on board it would help assure a safer flight in case of adverse weather or any in-flight difficulties. For the foreseeable future, Trippe was expecting to fly almost entirely over water, in his planned expansion of the mail routes to Central and South America.

Andre Priester was believed to be the first employee that Trippe hired and who reported directly to him. Priester's spe-

cialty was as a technical aviation and air safety expert. He became Trippe's right hand man and was a very powerful influence on him for many years. Priester began to immediately demand of Trippe, certain minimum safety requirements and tough new aircraft specifications. He insisted on multi-engines to insure dependable performance for all over water flights.

He also demanded and that's the key word, demand more of all the flight personnel especially in behavior. His plan was to project an image of PAA's flight crew as being a very confident, highly qualified group of healthy, well groomed gentlemen. He became exceptionally tough with the flight crews public image. He FIRED a pilot caught smoking in front of some passengers. There were similar incidents like this, where the Dutchman fired personnel on the spot if his policies weren't followed exactly. The good news about Priester was that he knew, from his European airline experience, how to run a rapidly expanding airline. It was felt that his judgement in most cases was very good and Trippe trusted him.

Leuteritz pushed Preister into getting radios and DF equipment aboard PAA's planes. It took a continuous effort on the part of Leuteritz to convince both Trippe and Priester that the flight tests he had been conducting proved that Capt. Fatt's serious crash in 1927, might have been avoided, if there had been working DF and two-way radio equipment on board that flight. Without dependable communications and navigating gear on board, more crashes could occur. So Priester, being interested in safety, issued an edict to install dependable air to ground transmitters, receivers and navigation aids aboard ALL

PAA's planes. His many edicts were supposed to give the future travelling public a greater feeling of confidence and security about flying with PAA. Adding better radio gear would certainly do that.

While Leuteritz worked for RCA developing Marine transmitters and receivers, his special interest was in the direction finding area. In 1927, Trippe hired him to consult for PAA in the DF equipment area. By 1929, Trippe had hired him away from CA. Trippe had him doing flight tests aboard the Fokker F7s flying between Key West and Havana. Leuteritz began to be famous for his ingenious problem solving methods. For example, the planes had no electric generators so he solved the problem by attaching a windmill type generator to a wing

UPPER LEFT: FRO Piere DeClaive smiles, while standing near the Boeing B307 Clipper Flying Cloud's tail section. He's waiting to board his flight to Rio de Janeiro. William Todd

UPPER RIGHT: PAA Captain Robert Fatt, Chief Pilot of the Latin American Division, piloting the B307 Stratoliner *Clipper Flying Cloud*. FRO was position behind the Skipper. 1939. PAA

BELOW: The Sikorsky S-40 NC81V docked at Dinner Key. Note, prior to departure, one of the beaching crew is washing windows as two others are holding the raft. Goreoke

ABOVE: The Sikorsky S-40 has just lifted off from Biscayne Bay on the most exciting flight of author Chapman's life.

LOWER RIGHT: FRO Ray Rielly in front of Port au Prince operations. He worked as the radio operator here as his foreign assignment. William Todd

strut. Another was the delicate radio parts were being shaken to pieces by the planes vibration so he suspended the equipment with ladies elastic garter belts which temporarily took care of that problem.

Capt. Bob Fatt (who later became Chief Pilot in Miami) and a few other early pilots were not a big booster of two way radio and particularly DF navigation. Admittedly there wasn't a lot known about DF limitations, such as the sunrise and sunset effect, when one could chase the bearings all over the dial and were inaccurate. The pilots hadn't learned to use and trust them yet.

The following quotation is a long one, and happened in 1927, but proves a big point as to just how reluctant or stubborn the early pilot group was to use any new devises. Capt. Fatt had the serious accident while Leuteritz was aboard doing radio flight tests. These tests should have proven that dependable two-way radios and particularly good DF bearings would have helped to prevented the crash. Quoting from Daley's "An American Saga" on Captain Fatt.

"Fatt took off from Havana on Aug. 15, 1927 at 3:55 PM, on the Fokker's return flight to Key West. Only the voice transmitter was working, the receiver was at Dinner Key being repaired. It was raining, visibility poor and the flight bumpy. They leveled off at 1,200. feet with a speed of 80 MPH with three passengers and mail were on board."

"At 4:55 PM, one hour out of Havana, the Fokker flew over a tramp steamer", Leuteritz radioed. They had not yet spotted Key West, he said.

"In his next transmission fifteen minutes later Leuteritz noted that all five men on the plane were peering out windows looking for the Sand Key Light. They could not find it. No one was yet very worried. "We did not see Cuba this morning until we were about five miles from it." Leuteritz said.

"We'll tell you when we see Sand Key Light, so stand by. He began to transmit every five minutes. The import of all these messages was the same.

ABOVE: This building is an example of many of the PAA line stations in the late '30s and early '40s and served as the flight operations and radio station at Port au Prince, Haiti. Note wind sock, anonometer and striped radio transmitter antenna masts.

BELOW: This is the radio station HHP's receiving equipment at Port au Prince. The station handled all arrival and departure radio traffic with the aircraft on flights between Miami and San Juan.

Visibility was poor. There was no sign of Key West yet."

"Two hours out of Havana Leuteritz radioed: Have not sighted the Keys yet. Passed a steamer headed same direction we are. We ought to sight something very soon now. Leuteritz kept radioing details: that Alfonso was peering around with binoculars, their air speed, as they dropped down to 1,800 feet, was about 100 MPH."

"Fatt, deciding that they must have missed the Keys to the east, turned northwest. Leuteritz radioed the change."

"For some time Priester, in the operations shack, had been standing first at Pippinger's shoulder and then at Sullinger's, listening to these messages. There was no alarm in Leuteritz's voice, but there was plenty in that shack. The experimental loop direction finder that Leuteritz had rigged to the roof of the shack was primitive, but it was sufficient to show that Fatt had just turned away from the Florida peninsula and was heading out into the Gulf of Mexico. Priester ran out of the shack and found Swinson, whom he sent up in the other plane to look for Fatt."

"Leuteritz, still transmitting, still did not sound particularly worried. At 6:16 PM, 2 hours 21 minutes out of Havana, he radioed another change of course. Think we allowed too much for drift, he said. . . When we get down to the last half hour of gas, we'll look for a ship and land near it." "From then on Leuteritz transmitted every two minutes:"

"Visibility poor, haven't sighted anything yet."

Things running smoothly. Have not sighted anything yet. Air calm. No whitecaps on the water. Have not sighted anything yet. Don't excite anyone, as everything is running smoothly. We intend to sight something before long. Have not sighted anything yet. Gas getting low. We are doing everything we can. Getting the boats ready."

"At Key West, Swinson was still out searching in wide circles. Visibility was as poor for him as for Fatt. Priester listening to every word from Leuteritz, now had two planes up there. He was worried about them both."

"At 6:52, 2 hours and 57 minutes out of Havana, Leuteritz began his final transmission. They had sighted a tanker below . . . Putting a note in a bay, Leuteritz radioed, getting ready to drop it to the ship."

"The tanker was the American Legionnaire. It was in some way airing out its tanks, and fumes that were invisible from the air hung over its decks. Alfonso opened his window and fired down an emergency flare. This created panic on the tanker. All its hatches were emitting fumes, into which an airplane was shooting fiery things. The crewmen were worried not about the Fokker's plight but about their own. As the General Machado swooped low over their decks a second time, Alfonso threw out his message inside a shirt tied to the inertial starter crank. If I am over 100 miles from land make a lot of black smoke. If I am less than 100 miles from land, turn your ship toward land."

"The crank handle landed in the water and sank."

"Fatt was circling, peering down, waiting for a response. None came. His left engine quit. Immediately he leveled off, and the engine started again. But on his next turn the right engine quit, and after it the other two. The General Machado, out of gas, glided down toward the sea. Fatt was trying to land as close as possible to the tanker. In August 1927 few pilots knew what a fixed gear airplane would do when it landed on water, particularly when a five to six foot sea was running.

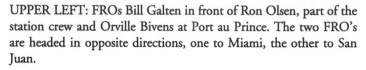

UPPER LEFT: FROs Bill Galten in front of Ron Olsen, part of the station crew and Orville Bivens at Port au Prince. The two FRO's are headed in opposite directions, one to Miami, the other to San Juan.

UPPER RIGHT: FRO Tommy Temple during ground crew training at Dinner Key in our official white coveralls with the red PAA initials over the pocket. The young bucks all thought they were "hot stuff" strutting around the hangar and terminal building. It was all so very exciting back then.

BELOW: FRO John Willmott, (Atlantic Airways, later became Pan American Air Ferries) with an ever present pretty girl? He was best man at my wedding. Photo credit goes to Johnny that showed a few of the many bombers that he and his Air Ferries buddies flew from Natal to Monrovia and other points in Africa during WW II.

off the gangway. There will be an investigation by the Department of Commerce, and if it turns out I am to blame, I'll never fly an airplane again."

"Press photographers moved forward. No, no pictures, said Fatt, holding his hands in front of his face. A flashbulb exploded anyway. Fatt grabbed the camera with his left hand and broke the photographer's jaw with his right. Five policemen jumped him, and he tried to fight them off. Then he was handcuffed."

"A lawyer sent by Trippe turned up, Fatt was released, and the survivors were sent back to Key West by boat. When they landed, Priester was there on the pier. If it makes things any easier for the company, Fatt told him, I will quit."

"Dere vill be an inwestigation, responded Priester. If you are to blame, you vill be fired. If you are not to blame, you vill be our most valuable pilot, because you vill be the only vun who ever landed on der vater." Later Fatt served as chief pilot on Pan American's Eastern Division for nine years.

Despite the crash, Preister remained lukewarm about navigation by radio . . .it was a radical idea and it was still unproven . . .and the pilots especially Fatt were totally opposed to it . . . This meant that navigation would pass outside the pilot's control altogether, and it constituted the worst heresy of all: the pilot in the air would be obliged to take orders from someone else."

After several months of hassle between Priester, the pilots and Leuteritz, a reluctantly agreed to plan was worked out. Leuteritz arranged with the pilots on each flight to Havana to have them hold the CW transmitter key down for a 10 or 15 seconds. He took bearings on the aircraft and radioed the pilots their latitude and longitude. They could do what they wanted to with the position report.

As mentioned earlier, in 1929 Trippe was able to finally woo Leuteritz away from RCA and put him on the payroll. He became the Communications superintendent, reporting directly to Trippe. Now that he had these two key people aboard, all of Trippe's dreams for conquering the airline world became more probable.

Johnny Wilmott is on extreme right with ferries crew in front of mileage board near Rabat. John Willmott

Chapter 4

I'm Hired, Met Flo

Now it's time to return to my main theme. Early on the morning of May 20, 1939, I found PAA's Communications Office in Coconut Grove. With my two FCC licenses in hand, I presented my serious New England face and accent to Elzian Bowers who interviewed me. After passing my physical, a code test and completing other paper work, I was offered the job. You can bet I happily accepted and started training May 22nd.

Thus began a wonderful period of my life as a young kid on a new venture. Looking back it seems to me that one of the happiest periods was the ten years I was with Pan American Airways (1939-49) I flew on the Clippers as a Flight Radio Officer. It was exciting, adventurous, fun and scary. But really what made it truly delightful and romantic was meeting, romancing, and marrying a dream. And what was the topping on my dessert was having a year's honeymoon with her on Rio's stunning Copacabana Beach. All compliments of Pan American's foreign assignment policy.

The fabulous young woman who caught my eye and sparked my romantic soul was Ms. Florence Ann Rodgers of Miami Beach. She worked at PAA's radio station WKDL at Dinner Key. She stopped me in mid stride, the first time I saw her at WKDL. I was stunned. I fell in love that moment and didn't know it. I wasn't to realize what had hit me until later. Much more on that soon. All I knew was I was at the right place at the right time and very happy to be there.

My starting salary was $125. a month. Annual vacation was 30 days. The only other benefit offered was health insurance. A special aspect of the employment application included an unusual requirement. It said that since PAA operated an international airline, employees were expected to readily accept foreign assignments to any place within the system for one to three years. This adventurous person was delighted to sign that proviso. I didn't know it at the time, that a transfer like that would suddenly move me into another world.

ABOVE: FRO Johnny Willmott transferred to pilot group in Atlantic Airways which became Pan American Ferries. He was a first officer pilot in this photo, on extreme left, with his bomber ferry crew. John Willmott

BELOW: Photo of bomber Johnny had just flown over the South Atlantic. John Willmott

UPPER LEFT: Master of Ocean Pilot Captain Richard Vinal at cockpit window of DC-6 in 1949. He was inducted into the Aviation Hall of Fame after 40 plus years of Naval aircraft carrier and Pan American Airways piloting over all the oceans and continents of the world. Vinal and Chapman had flown together in Rio in 1940 and many years later both families retired to Mercer Island, WA. A great pilot and special friend. John Willmott

UPPER RIGHT: Frank Chapman relaxes between flights in Botofogo Park, Rio. William Todd

LOWER RIGHT: FRO Arthur "Tiny" Moore and the author standing with Tiny's baby daughter in front of my apartment, the Edifico California on Copacabana Beach, Rio. Frank Chapman

PAA's training was continually changing but essentially complete, thorough, always safety oriented. I don't remember the exact order of my training. It included spending time in the hangar radio shop at Dinner Key Terminal. Jack Potter had me making 3 pound lead ball weights that were attached to the trailing antenna which improved radio signals while in flight.

We practiced manual radio direction finding procedures a lot. It was to be a very important requirement used whenever weather minimums prevailed at a landing site. We did this both aboard the Panair launch in Biscayne Bay and the Consolidated Commodore. Next came introduction to all the flight radio communications equipment. After that came life raft practice and other safety items. They gave me time to get acquainted with the paper work end of the job that included keeping flight logs and DF radio beacon charts that were kept on each leg of a flight.

If I recall correctly, Jack Potter and Popko were our friends in the radio shop, who we called on when we wanted to find out about any of the radio equipment. Earl "Pappy" Martin

was my flight instructor who then had the title of Chief FRO.

I was lucky on my initial flights and never forgot to reel in my trailing antenna before we landed. However there were several unnamed FRO's who forgot and had to spend two weeks grounded. They worked every day in the radio shop casting those ding dang lead ball weights. One poor fella had two or three forced visits to the radio shop before he got the message.

Pappy joined PAA in 1937, two years ahead of me. He seemed to me to have most of the answers to everything. He was a great instructor, really cool and was a very "with it" guy. We FRO's all liked him. I can remember his having several of us aboard the Commodore while it slowly droned around the Miami area at 1,000 feet. Each of us in turn had a crack at learning the instrument landing radio DF letdown procedure. Were we ever slow and kinda dumb I suppose, getting this new stuff into our sleepy heads.

We trained on the manual direction finder, the automatic direction finder had not been installed at the beginning. We

Performance Data on Aircraft Flown by Author

	Sikorsky S-38A	Sikorsky S-38B	Cons. Commodore	Sikorsky S-40	Sikorsky S40-A	Sikorsky S-42
Type	Amphibian	Amphibian	Boat	Amphibian	Amphibian	Boat
Length	40 feet	40 feet	68 feet	77 feet	77 feet	68 feet
Span	72 feet	72 feet	100 feet	114 feet	114 feet	114 feet
Wing Loading	-	-	-		-	28.5 lb/sq. ft.
Height	14 feet	14 feet	16 feet	24 feet	24 feet	17 feet
Gross weight	9,200 pounds	9,900 pounds	17,650 pounds	34,010 pounds	34,600 pounds	38,000 lbs.
Engines	P&W WaspX2	P&W HornetX2	P&W Hornet X2	P&W Hornet BX4	P&W Hornet T2DIX4	P&W Hornet X
Horsepower	410	450	575hp	575hp	660hp	700 hp
Range	595 statute miles	595 statute miles	1,000 statute mi.	800 miles	800 miles	1,200 miles
Fuel capacity	330 gallons	330 gallons	650 gallons	1040 gallons	1,060 gallons	1,240 gallons
Useful load	9,900 pounds	9,900 pounds	-	10,870 pounds	11,400 pounds	18,000 pounds
Cruising speed	112 mph	110 mph	102 mph	115 mph	120 mph	150 mph
Service ceiling	20,000 feet min.	19,000 feet min.	10,000 feet	13,000 feet	12,500 feet	16,000 feet
Climb rate	940 feet/minute	880 feet minute	-	712 ft/minute	712 feet/minute	800 feet per m
Passengers	8	8	22	34	40	38
Crew	3	3	4	5	6	5

would call out the bearings to the pilot so he could line up for the proper landing area and miss any nearby obstructions. Pappy was really patient with us. When we made a booboo, he'd give us that slow, shy smile of his and try to give us an encouraging word. We had to learn this routine perfectly as all our lives plus the passengers and the aircraft depended on giving the skipper the correct bearings for him to make a safe landing. We'd have to divert to our alternate airport if we didn't see water when we reached the airport minimums. I believe the typical minimum was 1000 ft ceiling and 1/2 mile visibility, for most landing areas. Some were only 500 ft and a 1/4 mile if there were no obstacles around.

For a week, I worked early mornings and evenings with the beaching crew. I'd don crisp white coveralls with the red letters PAA over the pocket. I was just young enough to proudly strut around the air terminal in those coveralls feeling important!

The beaching crew had to attach a heavy set of wheels under each docked Clipper. In this way any Clipper could be tractored up the ramp and into a hangar for maintenance. Work was needed after most flights. I was in and out of the water everyday. All of this explanation is to say that I got the worst case of athletes foot that stayed with me for years after. It was a bore.

When I first arrived at Coconut Grove, I found a nice boarding house across the street from Dinner Key terminal. It was run by "Ma Sawyer". I don't recall just how many FRO's she could house, probably 5 or 6. It was convenient. We didn't need any alarm clocks either since the ground maintenance crew would do engine runups before sunrise, on any aircraft that was outbound that day.

BELOW LEFT: Popular singer of WWII years, Grace Moore shown arriving at Rio's Santos Dumont Airport aboard a DC3, summer 1940. Frank Chapman

BELOW RIGHT: Aronha, our dependable Rio flight crew chauffeur, on the fender of his 1933 Packard touring car. He quickly and safely picked up each flight crew member prior to a flight and brought us to the airport and back home on our return. He used his horn often, to navigate us swiftly through the traffic jams of downtown Rio. He was very proud of his dirty white chauffeur's cap. He carried up to seven of us using the two jump seats. Frank Chapman

Sikorsky S-42A	Sikorsky S-42B	Sikorsky S-43	Martin M-130	Boeing 314	Boeing B314A
Boat	Boat	Amphibian	Boat	Boat	Boat
68 feet	68 feet	51 feet	90 feet	106 feet	106 feet
118 feet	118 feet	86 feet	130 feet*	152 feet	152 feet
29.9 lbs/sq.ft	31.3 lbs/sq. ft.	25 lbs/sq. ft.	-	-	-
17 feet	17 feet	18 feet	25 feet	28 feet	28 feet
40,000 pounds	42,000 pounds	20,000 pounds	51,000 pounds+	82,000 pounds	84,000 pounds
P&W Hornet X2	P&W Hornet X4	P&W Hornet X2	P&W Twin Wasp X4	Wright Cyclone X4	Wright Cyclone X4
750 hp	750 hp	750 hp	800 hp (later 800hp)	1500 hp	1600 hp
1,200 miles	1,200 miles	775 statute miles	3000 pass 4000 mail only	3,500 statute mi.s	4,275 statute mi.
1,240 gallons	1,240 gallons	690 gallons	4,000 gallons	4,200 gallons	5,448 gallons
18,000 pounds	18,000 miles	-	22,784 pounds	23,500 pounds	31,360 pounds
160 mph	155 mph	166 mph	157 mph	150 mph	150 mph
20,000 feet	15,000 feet	19,000 feet	20,000 feet	21,000 feet	21,000 feet
800 fpm	800 fpm	1,000 fpm	-	-	-
38	24	16/18	43 (as sleeper 18)	74 (34 at night)	74 (34 at night)
5	5	3	7	10-16	10-16

Chapter 5

Exciting Training on New Planes, New Horizons

Flights usually took off at sunrise so you can see we were awakened very early most mornings. I guess we were supposed to get used to the roar of engines. They seemed to be within feet of our bedroom windows. Yet all of this was part of the thrill and excitement of working for Pan Am.

Within weeks, I moved into an apartment at 3661 Palmetto Ave, Coconut Grove, with Charlie Chase and Oscar Olson. That was a great deal better, quieter and we had a kitchen to use. We actually got to be pretty good cooks although I tend-

CENTER RIGHT: The world famous crescent shaped beach front of Cocacabana Beach at Rio. The roof of author Chapman's apartment building can just be seen in bottom left corner, the Leme end. An old Brazilian fort is at the opposite end of the beach with many fine hotels and apartment buildings in between. Despite the often rough Atlantic Ocean surf the beach was often filled with bikini clad lovelies. Does anyone remember the song "The Girl From Ipanema?" William Todd

LOWER RIGHT: FRO Tommy Temple and his wife sit in front of the Edificio California apartment. Temple took Chapman's place when he was transferred to the Atlantic Division at La Guardia Field, New York. The Temples took over our apartment. Note the black and white mosaic sidewalk which was commonly used on the major Avenues. Frank Chapman

LEFT: Spectacular Igussu Falls located at the junction of three countries Paraguay, Brazil and Argentina was almost unknown by much of the world in 1940. The Captain flew over the falls on each flight into and out of Asuncion. Arthur Prado

BELOW LEFT: Avenida Atlantica mid-day traffic on Copacabana Beach.

BOTTOM LEFT: No swimming on that day, surf was much too high for a safe swim. Two photos by Frank Chapman

ed to make slightly different type sandwiches than what they liked. An example, I loved cold baked bean sandwiches, crushed pineapple and jelly beans, avocado and raisins. Don't those sound good to you?

About that same time, I was told to go get fitted for my uniform. Say, do you think I felt like King of the Mountain when I first put it on. You betcha. At this point, the company must have felt I was going to make the grade.

The communications and navigation equipment I learned about were the regenerative receivers, MOPA transmitters and loop, fixed and trailing antennas. In order to change frequencies, you had to swap plug-in coils which was kind of a nuisance. The first transmitters were only ten watts, yes, ten watts which was certainly peanut whistle power.

Pamsco was the company's own communications equipment designer and manufacturer headed by Leuteritz. It built gear that fitted our flight needs exactly. They produced an improved transmitter with 50 watts of power as well as receivers that had greater sensitivity and didn't require manually changing inductance coils to change to different bands of frequencies. Leuteritz was behind all these designs. At that point only Morse code was used, no radiophone. Effective air to ground voice radiophone over long distances was still a way off. What helped with our low power was usually we flew between 1,000 to 10,000 feet. The higher the altitude the better the signals were and thus gave longer distance communications. So it was easier to contact ground control stations 2,000/3,000 miles away depending on the frequency we used and the time of day.

The FRO rules were that we had to stay in contact with the departure or destination ground control station 100% of the

ABOVE: The *Yankee Clipper* "Queen of the Sky", NC 18603, a Boeing B-314, set a new standard for flying luxury accommodating 74 seated passengers and 34 at night. Twice the weight of a Sikorsky S-42, it cruised at 150mph, ten miles per hour less than the S-42.

BELOW: James Farley, U. S. Postmaster General standing by mail sacks about to be loaded aboard the Martin M130 *China Clipper* This inaugural airmail flight across the Pacific would join the West Coast of the United States with the Orient. The seven man flight crew included Captain Ed Musick and Captain Sullivan, Communications Superintendent veteran FRO Bill Jarboe, PAA's first master mariner and Navigator Fred Noonan, two top Flight Engineers C. D. Wright and Victor Wright along with George King, 2nd Pilot Officer. The flight left Alameda, California Nov. 22, 1935 headed for Manila with stops at Honolulu, Midway, Wake and Guam Islands successfully covering the 8210 miles across the Pacific in 59:48 flight hours to be greeted by a huge crowd in Manila harbor on Nov. 29, 1935.

Pan American Airways photos

time while in flight. Also we used the crude direction finding loop for taking bearings on lighthouse radio beacons or AM broadcast stations. These bearings were useful in showing us whether we were on our planned flight track, left or right. For example we could take bearings that checked our course direction. Other bearings that crossed our course, would give us our ground speed. This in turn would give us a position fix helping check our ETA.

Remember that this was a little before PAA had hired professional merchant marine navigators for any of the long over water flights. The pilots had to struggle with their time consuming celestial fixes or use dead reckoning. DF bearings the old time skippers continued to distrust.

Moving forward to late 1939, the company had given me two home study courses, meteorology and navigation. There was an interesting little kicker attached. We were told that completing the courses would make us better qualified FROs and a more valuable crew member. I found as soon as I'd finished both courses I got a raise to $140. a month.

Weeks stretched into months as I was given other aircraft to check out on and other countries and islands to fly to. As

The B314 *Yankee Clipper* NC 18603 leaving the coastline before WWII was declared, as the U. S. flag had not been painted on the bow. Note the small football shaped object atop the fuselage. This housed the radio direction finding loop used by the FRO as a supplemental aid to navigation by showing course direction and ground speed. Pan American World Airways

I mentioned the very first flight I had ever been on was aboard the Consolidated Commodore training flights over Miami with Pappy Martin.

I flew on board 14 different types of aircraft, during the ten years I was with Pan Am. That's a bunch. They included the Consolidated Commodore, Sikorsky S-38s, S-40s, S-41 S-42s, S-43s, Douglas DC-3s, DC-4s, Boeing B-307s, B-314s, B-377 and Lockheed L49s Constellations. I was on 314s for six years. From 1944 to 1946, we flew under Navy contract, (Naval Air Transport Service) often alternating between Navy and regular Pan Am flights. I flew aboard two more different planes, the Navy's PBY Catalina and the four engine Consolidated PB2Y3.

I spent a few weeks flying the Havana, Nassau and Cat Cay flights. After that I began to be assigned to all of the various other Caribbean Islands. For instance, I was assigned a flight to Merida, Mexico on an S-41, twin engined amphibian that cruised at 112 MPH. It was supposed to carry 8 passengers and a crew of 2. Because we had so much mail for that flight, the ground crew removed 4 seats. The rest of the space was full of mail bags. At this point in time mail was more important than passengers, it seemed. When I first saw the four passenger seats of the S-38 I wondered about them. I sat in one.

They were small, rickety, bamboo seats with no cushions. They were loosely fastened to the floor. I suspected that in case of a crash, all passengers would instantly have joined us two in the cockpit.

Going to Merida reminds me of the stories about mail versus passengers. When PAA started their operation from Key West, the only concern was getting the bags of mail delivered. The mail subsidy that PAA had negotiated with the Post Office Department was the company's only income. That first flight to Havana had seven sacks of mail, some 30,000. letters. Naturally they were most interested in how many pounds of mail they could carry at $2. a pound. I believe it wasn't until Priester came aboard that he reminded Trippe that more attention should be given to developing income from a bigger passenger base. He wanted to improve advertising which would remind people of the many advantages of flying and all the time it would save.

I didn't log the skipper's name on the Merida flight. Anyway I told him I was fascinated with flying and wanted to get my pilots license. Since I was the second and only other member of the crew aboard I asked him if I could help on the flight. He said sure. I worked the flaps on takeoff. We stopped in Cienfuegos, Cuba to unload the mail and a passenger. Then

The B314 cockpit was probably the largest sized of any aircraft built. It was 10 by 20 feet. The eleven man double crew was necessary to safely man the aircraft for 24 hours flight. The crew included the Captain in left seat, First Officer copilot right seat, Navigator and copilot standing at navigation table, Flight Radio Officer to Navigator's right and Second Flight Engineering Officer in right foreground. He had access to each of the four engines in flight via a catwalk in each wing. The balance of the eleven man crew included a second FRO, second Flight Engineer, a supernumerary pilot with two or three Stewards depending on passenger load. Pan American World Airways.

took off once more for the leg into Merida, Mexico. He actually let me fly straight and level on the last leg. Illegal as all get out I'm sure.

Sending code on that trip was very awkward, as I had the code key strapped to my thigh. This made it hard to send accurate dots and dashes while the tiny plane bounced and dipped in light turbulence. Come noon time I served the three passengers PAAs famous blue box lunches of unappetizing greasy, cold, tough chicken and rice. We also had luke warm bitter coffee. UGH!

Each time we landed I'd have to crawl under the instrument

RIGHT: FRO Floyd Hermanson shown taking a manual DF bearing. The FRO communications position consisted of two radio receivers that could be operated on either low or high frequencies. This meant the Flight Radio Officer was able to maintain constant radio contact with ground control stations throughout an entire Transatlantic flight sending aircraft position reports half hourly. The receiver frequencies covered from 200 to 18,000 kcs. At that time normal communications ranges were up to 3600 miles. In addition the FRO could take radio bearings automatically or manually on various vessels flown over or on AM radio broadcast stations and coastal beacons. Note the semi-automatic CW code key and typewriter for copying messages. William Todd

LEFT TOP: The twin engined Douglas DC-3 carried twenty to twenty eight passengers.

LEFT BELOW: In its sleeper configuration the DC-3 could sleep fourteen people in upper and lower berths, Pullman style.

TOP OPPOSITE: Pacific Northern AIrlines helped bring more dependable air service to isolated Alaskan communities

BELOW OPPOSITE: Douglas built the DC-3 at its sprawling plant in Santa Monica, California.
McDonald Douglas Archives

Chapter 9

A Real Spy Story- Delousing SCADTA

Before I describe our trip aboard the B-307, I feel there was a most unusual story that should be told about that particular plane. The story about the Flying Cloud, was a well kept war time secret that I learned much about. This Clipper, the Flying Cloud had already carved a place in history for itself.

I've taken excerpts of this highly secret story from Robert Daley's An American Saga, in chapter 39 "Delousing SCADTA". Here are some of the background facts on this fascinating true story.

Because of Trippe's exceptional foresight, in 1931, he had secretly negotiated with owner and chief executive Peter Paul

Von Bauer to purchase 85% of Columbia's airline SCADTA. He bought the shares for about one million dollars. This was part of his planned expansion into South America. It was mutually agreed between the two of them that Von Bauer would continue to operate the airline, keeping all the German employees. Secrecy was essential for both men but most particularly for Von Bauer. He had been a local national hero in Columbia, even had a statue erected for him in his honor. He had successfully established and run the airline for almost 20 years. SCADTA had opened up the mountainous inaccessible country to air travel which was appreciated by the Columbian government. For instance the capital, Bogota is at 8,400 feet elevation and had few connecting roads between its three high mountain ranges. Also it was Trippe's nature to keep these kinds of negotiations totally secret anyway. As you will see this secret purchase was kept from the general public for some time. The only concession that Trippe insisted on, was that Von Bauer should buy more modern, faster aircraft. Trippe forced Von Bauer into buying American DC-3's, which could carry more passengers, faster than the equipment SCADTA had. In the 1931 annual report Trippe did cryptically announce to the stockholders that "PAA had acquired substantial interests in SCADTA". But few people knew just how extensive that was.

Now in 1939, with war looming, Trippe was forced to testify before a State Department hearing. He finally told the committee just how much PAA was involved. He admitted that for all practical purposes PAA owned SCADTA. When this became public, many people in State Department were badly disturbed. In fact the American ambassador to Columbia, Spruille Braden, was outraged. He felt that for eight years PAA had permitted the Germans to run the airline so close to the Panama Canal that it was just short of treason. Braden along with Gen. David Stone, Canal Zone commandant, flooded Washington with messages demanding the

"Mr. Jones" (President Roosevelt) aboard a B314 Clipper enroute to Casablanca summit with Churchill. He enjoyed his 61st birthday somewhere over the South Atlantic between Natal, Brazil and Fisherman's Lake. His aides were Admiral Leahy and Harry Hopkins with PAA Captain Howard Cone right foreground. This was an ultra secret special flight #71, 1943. Pan Am Historical Foundation

Washington direct but also stated that he would not proceed unless President Santos concurred as well. The CAB also got into the act and agreed to pay $250,000 to Pan Am to cover costs of German repatriations, under the heading of "national defense".

Del Valle, Pan Am's spy, was ordered to New York. He found fully qualified flight crew applicants had been assembled there and he hired 35 on the spot. The problem was how to smuggle these people into Colombia without SCADTA suspecting anything. Again, Trippe the master planner, had come up with a plan in detail. Enter the Boeing Clipper Flying Cloud center stage.

"A Boeing Stratoliner, NC 19903 Flying Cloud was the world's first four-engined high altitude pressurized landplane, had just been delivered; two more were to follow. When it took off for Columbia on June 3, 1940, supposedly on a gala introductory flight and tour of South American capitals, it carried all the pilots and technicians that Del Valle and others had hired. The plane landed at Barranquilla first, and then at Bogota, and during the civic celebrations that ensued, pilots and technicians sneaked away from the airports and were hidden in various hotels."

On June 12, 1940 all was ready to put Plan B into operation and Rihl sent out a coded message to that effect. Del Valle called a SCADTA maintenance meeting at Barrinquilla At exactly 5 PM, he began a speech and was not at ease. This was war, he said. He was not personally responsible for any of this and handed out the 85 letters of dismissal and severance paychecks. The assembled Germans were stunned, some had tears in their eyes. They protested that they were Columbians and didn't deserve this kind of treatment. President Santos had Columbian troops already placed at all of SCADTA installations around the country. The Germans were not allowed to return to the shops and get their personal effects but were forced to leave the building immediately.

The next morning the American flight crews took over the flight schedule and resumed service, without losing a day. Rihl sent a coded message to Trippe: "Plan B successful".

How is that for some behind the scenes spy story?. I certainly hadn't known about any of that was going on. Such intrigue! And too, what a far sighted planner Trippe was.

Sikorsky S-37 Pan American Clipper, NC8000, arriving at the Canal Zone with the first airmail from Miami, Florida with Colonel Charles A. Lindberg commanding, Feb. 8, 1929 only two years after his historic solo flight across the Atlantic Ocean. This Sikorsky S-38, is believed to be the first one PAA purchased Oct 31, 1928. Pan American World Airways

Chapter 10

Honeymooning in Rio! Rio Based Crews

Reading an old letter I had written my folks in early August 1940, I had said "Did you see the PAA Boeing B-307 Stratoliner on the front cover of the Saturday Evening Post of August 17, 1940? That was the plane I was on, that made the first passenger flight to Barranquilla". That was the Flying Cloud, since the other two B-307s had not yet been delivered. I suspect my flight there was only weeks after the SCADTA takeover, yet I was totally unaware of all the intrigue that had just finished. Did any of you FROs know about it?

After sitting on about nine suitcases to close them and get-

ting them breathlessly to the check-in counter, Flo and I stared out at what seemed like a huge plane sitting on the runway. As we climbed aboard the Clipper Flying Cloud, B-307 Stratoliner that August 28th morning, we found that it not only looked big but was BIG inside with great soft and roomy seats. As I recall, seating on one side of the plane, there were several clusters of two pairs of seats facing each other, like on a Pullman car. None of the passengers wanted to fly backwards! On the other side, seats all faced forward.

At long last we were airborne. Captain Max Weber had lifted off the runway so smoothly, I hardly noticed it. We were on our way to Rio and new adventures. I know we were holding hands and excitedly wondering what lay ahead, how many things had we forgotten and all that. On that first leg we flew non-stop to San Juan. It took only 5:47 minutes. That was very speedy, compared with the average flight time in a an S-42 of 8:32 minutes plus over 3 hours on the ground at Port au Prince and Santa Domingo!

When Flo and I arrived in San Juan we were still dazed from all the hurried preparations to move. We checked in at the Condado Hotel. I was delighted to show Flo around this luxury beachfront hotel. That night we went to the Escombrom Club where she and I danced until almost dawn. That whole transfer was a thrilling adventure for we two young kids of 20

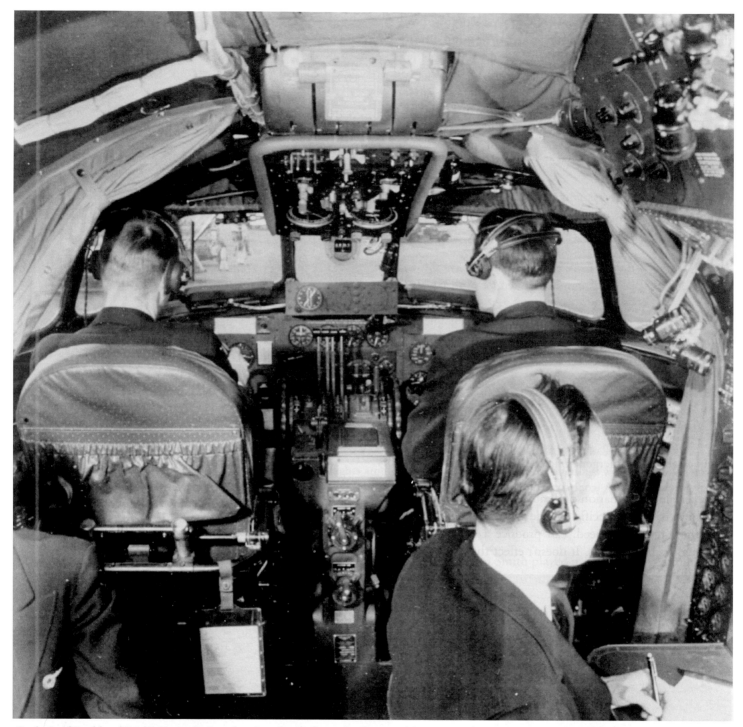

Cockpit of Lockheed L049 Constellation showing the flight crew. Circa 1946. Some airlines carried a fourth flight crew member: a Flight Engineer. Compare the Connie's cockpit with those in much simpler Sikorsky aircraft from an earlier period. Lockheed Martin Archives

mit from the plane.

The roaring built so that no matter where I tuned the receiver dial I got a loud roar in my ear phones. Of course this made it impossible to hear any incoming voice transmissions or beacons. Without our radio or DF working correctly, we quite literally were flying blind. So I called the alternate field radio station, in the blind. I asked the radio station operator to turn on his emergency generator and beacon as we had diverted from BA. Our ETA at their field was in twenty five minutes. A very short notice to get a normally unmanned field

ready for a plane arrival.

The strip chart of the field showed a minimal length grass strip, no lighting and emergency radio beacon on request. I had started to call this field as soon as we had turned back north but that is when the static roar completely covered all incoming signals. So I didn't know whether he had received my message or not. I repeated my message several more times with no audible reply.

Finally the static roar began diminishing and I could hear him calling me. He said the beacon was on but I still couldn't

FRO Frank Chapman was aboard the PAA inaugural flight from New York to Johannesberg, South Africa, that took off Feb. 25, 1948 and returning to LaGuardia Airport on March 8, 1948. Author Chapman is at the radio operating position with two BC348 receivers, two multichannel 150 watt Collins transmitters, two ADF receivers and a LORAN navigational equipment. The flight was on a Lockheed L049, NC 88857 *Flying Mist*. This historic flight carried 20 prominent U. S. newspaper and magazine editors. Pan Am Historical Foundation

hear it yet. In a few minutes it began building to a strong signal above the moderate roar. That told me we were close to the station as I had to turn the volume down fast.

I shouted to the skipper a bearing to steer and told him it sounded close and we were about to fly directly over the beacon. He started descending rapidly. The copilot said he saw a cow pasture full of cows below and we wondered if that was the field. We circled what we thought was the field, at tree top level and agreed yes it was where we were to land. The skipper began some tight banking circles over the cows to get them into a corner. About that time a truck appeared and began herding them out an open gate while we slowly circled. Then the skipper lined up for the narrow runway and did a great short field landing with a crabbing stall attitude. Then stood on the brakes hard and slid to an abrupt halt on the grassy runway. The fence was only a few feet away. He turned the engines off quickly. We three just sat there, in the silence, listening to the engines make their cooling down ticking sounds. I suspect we each threw a quick prayer into the air and said "thanks Lord". I know I did.

It took us hours to arrange to get the 55 gallon drums trucked to the pasture/field, only to find that their gas pumps were too weak to pump the gas up 20 feet to the wing tanks. So more time was lost while a bigger pump was found. In the

mean time I was at the radio station listening to the BA weather which hadn't improved at all. I told the skipper this. He elected to tell the passengers we'd we overnighting in this whistle stop place. I seem to recall I volunteered to sleep on the plane and be a watchman as well. The bottom line is my log book said we got out the next morning and arrived in BA without further incident.

I admit I can't find the name of this hick town where we had landed 54 years ago. I don't have copies of those old DF maps we used to use. Even then it probably wouldn't have the alternate field listed. Someone of you old FROs* just might have a Panair do Brazil chart of 1940 that would show it. Who knows. Let's face it back then, some of the less technically advanced countries didn't always provide safe landing areas. *(PS: Art Prado recalled that the name of the field was MONTE CASEROS)

That year in Rio was the least safe flying conditions I ever flew in. I feel all of us flight crews were so very young and bold, and maybe even fearless most of the time. We believed all would be okay. "It couldn't happen to me" kind of attitude. We seldom talked about being afraid especially during a flight. Later, after landing and over a coffee, we might say "Wow, that was some frontal conditions we went through" and that would be it. I believe we all were fatalistic. If trouble happened, we

Rio flight to only 3 days instead of the usual 5 via the coastal route. The B-307 had made an inaugural flight from Miami to Panama also, 1,200 miles non-stop in 6:30 minutes.

I took the same route on a DC-3 but stopped to refuel at Barreiras a halfway point. It seemed they didn't know what was going on, as we were the first planes to use that stop and the ground facility wasn't completely ready for us. I later found out the company's arrangements were complicated, All materials for the airport had had to travel by rail from Belem and then on a barge on the San Francisco river for 750 miles. Also they had to barge several hundred 55 gallon drums of aviation fuel, from the coast near Maceio. I don't know how many days that project had taken. Anyway, once they got to the base of the plateau, PAA's ground crew had to bring the fuel drums up the side of the plateau on a donkey, two at a time. That had to be a really slow process. Flight time from the log was 8:21 minutes to Belem. It was certainly better than the coastal route of two days. My return flight to Rio was 8:43 minutes. The faster planes did make a difference. I don't have a record of the flight time between the Canal Zone and Belem, probably 7 or 8 hours.

When you look at a map of Brazil, you can see the direct route from Belem takes you over the central part of the country called Mato Grosso Plateau. In the middle of all this nothingness is Barreiras and it's at the junction of three rivers, the biggest of which is the Rio Grande. An airport was built on top of a tiny flat plateau about two miles long and a mile or so wide, with an altitude of 1,300 feet. A wee small settlement of a hundred people, lived at the river junction. The airport was opened by a DC-3 first and immediately followed by a B-307.

Son Allan Arrived, Aug. 4, 1941

We were destined to stay in Rio for only a little over a year, because things were heating up in Europe. The company elected to beef up the flight crews in the Atlantic Division. It was necessary to rotate some of the crews from Rio to New York and I was on that list.

Because we were expecting a baby, Flo's German doctor suggested she fly back to Miami around the seventh month, which she did. Allan Westcott Chapman arrived on Aug. 4, 1941, at Miami Beach. I was so elated with Allan's arrival but angry with PAA. The company had said they had transfer rotation problems and I always regretted not being present at our first child's birth. But that's life.

Chapter 15
Joined Flo, Baby Alan in New York

It was Oct. 2, 1941, when I found myself aboard a northbound flight to Miami and an introduction to Allan and my beautiful wife whom I hadn't seen for two whole months. What a deeply moving and exciting moment it was to see Florence again and get a look at my two month old handsome son and hold him lightly in my arms. Even now 53 years later, I feel a warm thrill of pleasure about that moment. Flo was an absolute gem and had written me almost daily, super love letters but obviously it wasn't like hugging that warm lovely body, in person.

We three left Miami soon after and settled into an upstairs unfurnished apartment in a private house on Elm St., Glen Cove, Long Island. We rushed out and bought a bed, crib and I think that was all we could afford at that moment. I seem to remember having several orange crates around that Flo had covered with some of our fine linen table clothes. She was always a great home maker and interior decorator. But we didn't have living room furniture for a little while. Now we were back in a big metropolitan area where we didn't have to worry about drinking water or eating raw vegetables. And of course, there was our satisfying Coca Cola available everywhere. Everyone spoke English, too. I got my months vacation that all flight crews got so it gave us time to settle in well. Pan Am's flights across the Atlantic had begun to expand dramatically due to the war.

I was introduced to the most beautiful aircraft, the Boeing B-314 seaplane. It was called the "world's greatest". My first flight in the Atlantic division was a training flight of 1:46 minutes aboard the B-314. Pan Am's new terminal was built alongside La Guardia airport and the Coast Guard marine base with the landing area at the very western end of Long Island Sound. The area was called North Beach near Flushing.

First, let me describe the crew makeup and the plane, as it was so very different from what I had been flying. We had an eleven man crew, consisting of Captain McCullough, three pilots, two Flight Radio Officers, two Flight Engineers, a Navigator and two Stewards. With this number in the crew we could stay aloft up to 24 hours.

The B-314 was the greatest seaplane of its type in the world. It certainly was the biggest seaplane ever used for regular commercial flight service. It could carry between 35 and 74 passengers depending on several factors.

Everything was first class, no economy or coach class. It had a 15 seat dining lounge, and a galley where complete hot meals could be prepared from scratch, by the Stewards. The passenger lounges had davenport type chairs with carpeting and sound proofing throughout. The women's powder room had

President Trippe presents Captain Hugh Gordon with United Nations flags of countries Clipper America where stops were planned on the first round-the-world passenger flight in history. This was at La Guardia Airport, N. Y. just before takeoff on June 17, 1947 on a new Lockheed Constellation L049 N88858. At far left is Mayor Roger Lapham of San Francisco and Mayor William O'Dwyer of New York. Pan American World Airways

primping stools and large mirrors and the men's room had the first and last in commercial aviation—twin urinals along with over-the-ocean disposal. The luxury didn't stop there, there was even a deluxe honeymoon suite in the tail.

It could sleep up to 40 passengers, plus crew bunks for four. It had the longest range of any flying boat ever built, 4,275 miles and could cruise at 150 MPH. A never-ever exceed red-line was 184 MPH. Operating ceiling was 16,000 feet and powered by four 1600 HP Wright Cyclones. Its fuel capacity was 5,400 gallons, a lot of it was carried in the two sponsons or sea wings used to give more stability on the water.

The cockpit was an upper deck the crew got to via circular stairs and was probably the biggest flight deck ever designed by any aircraft manufacturer, about 10 by 20 feet with walkways out into the wings, for easy access to the engines in flight.

The Flight Radio Officer sat six feet behind the copilot and directly opposite the navigation table. A few feet behind the FRO was the Flight Engineer's station. The crew bunks were directly below the cockpit and next to the galley and was reached by the spiral staircase. The radio equipment was much the same as we had been using in Rio.

When the company transferred us, we found ourselves moving from a rather special world famous beach in a foreign city which was somewhat out of the main stream of world affairs, to the New York City area that put us smack into the middle of world war preparations.

Chapter 16

World War II Began, First Mid-Atlantic Flight To Lisbon

A moment of history now. The Atlantic Division essentially began the first scheduled airmail flights May 20, 1939. (That is when I was just being hired in Miami). That flight carried 200,000 letters which flew from New York to Marseilles via Horta and Lisbon. The regular three times a week passenger schedule began a month later, June 28. These flights had been taking off from Manhasset Bay in Port

85

Washington, L.I. and cost $375 one way or $675. round trip.

There had been a game played between PAA and the British as to who would be ready first to have a regular service across the Atlantic. Trippe had agreed with BOAC that each would wait so the flight service across the Atlantic could begin simultaneously. PAA won. BOAC had run into all kinds of complications, mainly equipment failures and weather. Claire Booth Luce wrote about her first flight "50 years from now people will look back upon a Clipper flight of today as the most romantic voyage of history".

A year and a half later on Dec. 11, 1941, I was about to climb aboard the NC18604, the Boeing B-314 Atlantic Clipper, for the first time. It would be my first flight in the Atlantic Division. It had just dawned on me that we were at war. This meant that lots of schedules, destinations and other concerns required many adjustments on our part. Flo's and my little world of Rio, on the beach, had changed dramatically to the big real world of Long Island and greater New York City. I thought about the differences; language, changing seasons, familiar food, Coca Cola, nearer our families, the new load of responsibilities with Allan, owning a car again, learning new procedures on the biggest commercial aircraft in the world and trying to live on my salary. Our savings ability had stopped. And we were expecting food and gasoline rationing. But being the eternal optimist, I dove into the new life with enthusiasm and happy energy, delighted with our new family member Allan. . . and my beautiful loving wife who continued to be a great support in all ways.

I was now going to fly aboard a huge, long range aircraft that would sometimes keep me out of the country up to 30 days at a time. That was a long time to be away from my family but that was the way it was then, I'd grin and bear it

Captain McCullough and the rest of us marched on board the early evening flight on Dec. 11th, which was to be my first night flight as well as my longest trip of my career so far. It would be 86:02 flight hours, taking 9 days and covering 10,861 miles. We'd land in six countries and seven different cities. It was called the "O" trip where we flew across the mid Atlantic to Lisbon and returned to New York via the South Atlantic. Portugal would remain neutral throughout the war.

Since transferring to the Atlantic Division, I found each flight crew on the B314 would include a Navigator. He was responsible for preparing all hourly position reports to be sent to the airport radio station handling the flight watch. He'd supply the correct headings and ETA for the skipper too. In order to do this properly, he had to have clear sky overhead to take star sights with his Octant. By taking these sights and noting the time accurately, he'd mathematically calculate the plane's position. Each hour the FRO would send this message to the company's flight operations department via the radio station guarding the flight. A three star fix was always preferred as it was far more accurate but often took 10 minutes or more to calculate.

Also, the Navigator had to see the ocean below so he could drop his flares or smoke bombs in the water. He'd peer through the telescopic drift sight in the keel, to see which direction the wind was blowing the smoke, and estimate the speed. It was a rough estimation but the best available at that point in time.

Obviously it was important to know the direction from which the wind was coming from, and its force. It effected the plane's course and speed over the water or ground in some manner. Engine RPM's control the air speed only, but the wind effects the ground speed and direction. So the wind coming from either side of the plane could push it off course left or right. But if it was a head wind the plane's ground speed would be slowed. On the other hand if the wind were a tail wind, of course the planes speed over the water would be increased. As you can see, it was essential that each flight keep track of the wind direction and force at all time.

When a flight was in overcast weather the Navigator would have to use dead reckoning navigation, supplemented with radio bearings supplied by the FROs. This happened pretty regularly. Radio bearings were quickly and easily taken and were reasonably accurate, assuming the radio station signal was strong and it wasn't sunrise or sunset which could caused unsteady signals. The FROs also used Coast Guard ships on Atlantic patrol and nearby passenger ships to take bearings on. This later method was halted soon after I arrived, due to eminent buildup of German subs in the Atlantic. I was glad for their weather information and bearings but I felt sorry for the crew on weather ship "Charlie". I was told they had to spent six months duty tossing, rocking and rolling on those little CG "Tin cans".

A word about FROs Jim Sanner and Vic Johnson. Before they were ever assigned to flight duty and the upcoming flight with me, they had completed all the same kind of training I had had in Miami. In addition they spent hours in a new radio direction finder simulator called a "DF Link trainer" similar to what the pilots used for practicing instrument landings.

They had also been given all the communications and DF data needed for a given flight. As an example, on this flight both Jim and Vic would have been given the call letters and frequencies of all the flight control radio stations as well as useful commercial radio broadcast stations and beacon identifiers near our flight path. Essentially, either of these men could have flown the routes alone but as always the company was cautious and trained their flight crews well.

The log book I have been referring to off and on is my own personal flight log book which only has the flight date, aircraft number, type plane, airport three letter code, Skipper's name, FROs names, flight times, and remarks. I've kept this log all these years. On the other hand, PAA's communications logs and DF flight charts of each flight were turned into the company long ago, and are probably in Pan Am heaven. They contained all the minute details of each air to ground radio contact, weather report, time signal received and each bearing taken. So anything I put down here on call letters of control stations are from memory. So some data may be inaccurate, isn't that the usual disclaimer?

At long last the skipper began taxiing slowly out into Flushing Bay headed for the takeoff area. I was intently watching the various red and green lighted buoys, La Guardia Field, white runway lights, the control tower's red flashing light and of course New York's famous skyline. I was anxious to take in all the new night sights. After everyone had completed their check lists, we turned into the wind. Capt. McCullough told the copilot to adjust the flaps and to slowly push the throttles forward. We quickly moved onto the step. In 30 seconds we had the right airspeed and the skipper pulled back on the yolk and we gently took off with a great roar from the four powerful Wright Cyclones that produced 6,400 HP.

We took up a southeasterly course for Hamilton, Bermuda, 770 miles away. The throttles were pulled back to 1,900 RPM for our climb to cruising speed of 150/170 MPH. Our altitudes would vary on each leg depending on winds aloft, clouds and freezing levels. Eastbound across the Atlantic we would usually climb to 7,000/10,000 feet as there was a good prevailing tail wind at the higher altitudes that speeded us along.

From my flight log, this circle trip listed two Flight Radio Officers beside myself: Jim Sanner and Vic Johnson. They had just finished their ground training and as senior man, I was to check them out on this flight. The demand for crews had jumped dramatically because of the U. S. war effort

I told Jim and Vic, I would take the first leg to Bermuda. I asked them to come up on the flight deck every hour and I'd show and tell on what I'd done.

As we climbed to cruising altitude, I tuned in the time signals from Greenwich, England and told the Navigator how many seconds his chronometer was off. All international airlines, ships and the military ran on Greenwich Mean Time (GMT) and this is what the Navigator used for his celestial fixes.

I began taking a series of DF bearings on broadcast radio stations. First I used WEAF, N. Y. to check our flight track, then tuned in WBAL, Baltimore and WTAR, Norfolk to confirm our ground speed. I'd plot these bearings on my own DF chart as well as giving them to the Navigator to add to his mas-

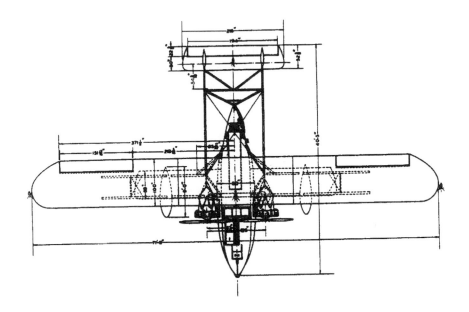

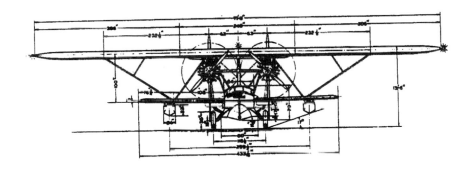

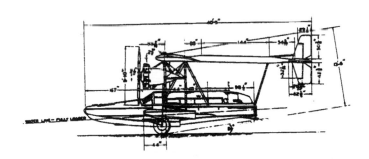

Three view of Sikorsky S-38B

ter chart of our flight. This was a double check on his fixes.

Two hours after takeoff, La Guardia Radio turned the flight watch over to radio station VRT in Bermuda on 3285/5692 khz. I requested an update on weather and landing conditions and handed it to the skipper. The weather was fine. I took DF bearings on his low frequency signal to confirm that our flight path was on track. Continued to home in on his signals which were coming in strong. Jim and Vic came to the flight deck several times and seemed to be absorbing everything well. This leg had been easy for them but we'd share the next leg to Horta.

Another first for me. Standing between the two pilot's seats and looking out and up gave me a truly inspiring and brilliant display of God's beautiful heaven of stars and planets. I was even able to identify several: Mars, Dubbe, Venus . . . from my recent Navigational studies. We flew smoothly along under the brilliant night sky until we lightly touched down in Castle Harbor, 4:44 minutes flight time from New York.

After letting off any passengers, unloading mail and refueling, we normally would have departed within an hour or so after landing. For some reason I didn't note, we overnighted there.

In the morning, we had an hour's test flight. My guess is that we had had some minor engine fault, probably rough plugs or damp ignition wires. There were a double set of spark plugs and harnesses and dampness in either plugs or harness could cause an unacceptable drop in RPM's when the mags were checked before takeoff. We all had been taught, take all prudent safety precautions before proceeding on any long overwater flight; and if there was any doubt, cancel the flight. Let the passengers moan. It was carefully spelled out in Priester's flight manuals.

The second day we took off for Horta, in the Azores at sunset, 1,822 miles away. It was a long night and a very smooth flight, taking us 13:44 minutes This is the leg when we FRO's did our split watches. I had Jim and Vic take the first two four hour watches and I handled the last one into Horta.

A two letter initialing system was used on the air to acknowledge who had sent or received the messages aboard the plane. Here's an example of a few I recall. Bivens, OB; Chapman, FC; Conly, VT; Chase, CS; Martin, PM; Mason, LM; Mathews, GF; Prado, HP. The reason I'm mentioning this two letter sign system is that my log book normally indicated who flew with me as the second FRO on our B314 double crew. That's how I identified Jim, NN and Vic ON on this flight.

There's nothing in my log about treacherous swells at Horta Bay but I need to mention them here now as they had caused accidents and numerous delays in the past. The cause of the varying swell conditions seemed to have been due to the geological settling of the volcanic islands of the Azores, eons ago. The water in the bay where we landed had a shallow dropoff which was conducive to producing rather vicious swells at times. I believe they were caused by a combination of wind direction, force and tides in the shallow bay and were measured in feet. Normal swells ran between 3 to 5 foot crests. We could land or take off in those conditions. However, if the swells were any higher we couldn't land or if the swells deteriorated while we were docked, we'd be delayed until the swells lessened. Was that any way to run an airline?

That morning we landed okay and began refueling while the passengers went ashore and did a bit of shopping for straw hats or Port wine both of which were tourist items.

An interesting incident happened a year earlier when Captain Sullivan's flight had troubles with the Horta swells. He had a load of newspaper publishers on a publicity flight to

Europe and was returning to New York. When he landed at Horta, a maverick swell stove in the bow. It was a fairly minor accident but the landing caused a serious leak in the hull. Sully believed in landing an aircraft flat and fast, instead of the more normal steeper and slower method used by most of the other pilots.

There's a saying among those who fly that there are old pilots and there are bold pilots, but there are no old, bold pilots. Sully leaned toward the bold side. A former Naval aviator, he was known for his tendency to fly aircraft with a heavy hand on the controls. I had flown with him several times while based in Miami and I concur. I'll take an excerpt from Robert Daley's "Saga" about Sully here, as it is appropriate.

Sully's accident he had at Horta, was blamed on a "maverick swell" although some wanted to blame Sully. Priester happened to be on Sully's flight and was frightened that the news media would blow the accident all out of proportions.

Priester immediately arranged a side trip for the publishers to another island in the chain while he frantically made plans to correct the problem. He than telephoned Capt. Harold Gray in New York and had him fly a replacement B-314 to Horta. Two days later Gray had the publishers back in New York on the replacement plane. No news leak either. How the company did all this without making the newshawks curious was a mystery to me but it happened.

Gray had insisted that Sully's accident was not pilot error but in fact was probably a design fault of the B-314 keel. Gray urged that Boeing investigate. Boeing found that by extending the hull step aft by 20 inches, water handling characteristics definitely improved. So retrofit kits were supplied and added to the B-314 fleet. After that they performed like pussycats on the water.

Now back to my flight where we were ready to take off for Lisbon. We took off again right away without a problem with the swells. It sometimes took a special but careful technique by the skipper, of bouncing, and not so gently either, from crest to crest in order to lift off by yanking back on the wheel at the right moment and hope the airspeed was high enough to keep us airborne. Kind of tricky really. Captain McCullough had that technique down pat.

The 1082 miles to Lisbon was smooth and without incident and took us 6:24 minutes. About midway on this leg, I changed the CW flight watch to radio station CTV and got the usual weather report that I passed on.

Later, as we approached the coast of Portugal, I realized I had mixed feelings; joy, excitement, but with some apprehension. I was delighted to be arriving at a new city and happy to get a taste of Portugal for the first time. But also I was a shade concerned about the war situation and what was going to happen. Even though the war front was several hundred miles away, it seemed much closer than I wanted to be. I know I had regularly tuned in to BBC news broadcasts each night so as to keep the crew and me informed. I don't recall what was actually happening at that moment but I personally didn't feel very comfortable about it.

While the skipper landed on the Tagus River and taxied up to the dock, I anxiously looked around. I don't recall what I expected to see but actually saw nothing unusual so began to feel more relieved. The pier we were tied to was in the midst of a lot of activity; passengers ships, ferries, and small fishing vessels all around us in the broad Tagus.

Chapter 17

In Love With Fascinating Lisbon

After clearing immigration and customs we walked to a taxi. We were told we'd be staying in a downtown Lisbon hotel called the Aviz. It had been a palace with 20 bedrooms before it had been converted into a hotel. When we checked in I found it charming and luxurious. But when I got to my bedroom I found just what real luxury was all about. The room was large and beautifully decorated with a huge canopied bed, lovely paintings and mirrors everywhere. Even a sunken bath totalled mirrored. It seemed like what I imagined a bordello would look like, red curtains and all. I got to see my first douche, sitting along side the regular toilet with gold fixtures. I exclaimed at dinner that I had never experienced such luxury and got a bit of kidding from the rest of the crew. I lost track of the number of courses we ate.

Some of my first impressions I got when we were driven to the hotel were varied of course. First, Lisbon was a busy, bustling, large city of about 2,000,000 people with narrow, crowded cobblestone streets. Colorful brick houses with bright red tiled roofs, were crowded against each other. Flower pots and bird cages were hanging everywhere. Women walked along carrying baskets on their heads, donkeys carrying milk, door to door. It was a hilly city and one of the crew said it was built on seven hills much like San Francisco.

The taxi driver, I thought, was crazy. He drove recklessly, speeding through intersections while he blew his horn energetically for everyone to get out of his way. Later I found that most taxis were driven in that cavalier manner.

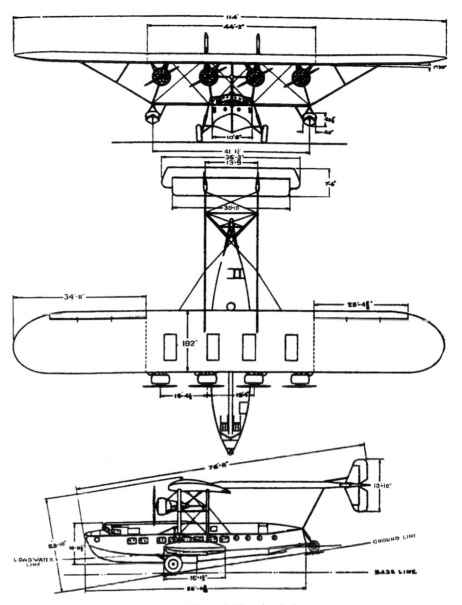

Three View of Sikorsky S-40

When we got closer to downtown, the streets broadened into lovely wide boulevards with spectacular flower gardens in the center median. I was told that the flowers bloomed almost all year because the climate was so moderate. All the sidewalks were exactly as I'd seen in Rio, black and white stone mosaics. The overall sensation when I arrived downtown was of beauty and I've never changed my love for that city and Portugal in general.

The people turned out to be a delight, genuinely warm and friendly. As I've said, Portugal was neutral, so over the next five years I would find myself spending a lot of layover time in this lovely city. with its thousands of attractive red tiled roof buildings. The central business district was a most interesting mix of buildings and roads.

There were hundreds of smaller hills everywhere, so building lots weren't always flat. Also roads and streets stopped and started every which way. What I'm trying to say here is that it was difficult for me to find my way around the city when I

of a child and all the preparations of welcoming a new member into the family. I impatiently waited around in the hospital corridor for something to happen. The Doctor finally came out to say that Florence was fine but that I should go on home as things were progressing nicely but slowly.

I left feeling kind of useless and left out of everything. And of course I was at that moment. So I went home to bed. It seemed only a short time later when the telephone awakened me with the message that at 2 AM I had become a father again. Son Kenneth Frank Peter Chapman had arrived. I felt so damn proud even though Flo had done all the work!

Shortly afterwards, I found myself at the hospital peering through the nursery window at this incredibly tiny creature who was my son. If I had had an old style vest on I would have burst all the buttons, in pride. Still later when I saw Flo feeding him and I got to hold him and burp him, I realized once again, this was what love and marriage was all about. I was feeling humble seeing another one of God's miracles and I felt oh so very happy.

Chapter 21

The Navy Calls

People used to ask me what I did during World War II. I suspect that my answer was usually sort of vague. As you know I flew for PAA from 1939 until 1949 and remained on their payroll all during that period. At the time we didn't know what was going to happen because the draft board had started calling some of Trippe's precious flight crews to active duty. And he certainly wouldn't permit that he said.

I later found out that there had been many meetings between Trippe, the War Dept. and Franklin D. Roosevelt, as to what to do with the "Chosen Instrument" as Pan Am was referred to. After much heated discussion a consensus was reached. The PAA flight crews would be taken into the Naval Air Transport Service (NATS) and therefore the flight crews would remain intact. Trippe and we were happy about that arrangement.

At the time we were told very little as to just what was happening. But one day in May we were told to report to the Navy enlistment center at Grand Central Railroad Station in New York. When we arrived in the city to register along with thousands of other young guys, we sat and fidgeted, wondering what was next.

With continuous announcements over the PA system and lots of signs we crept along from area to area. We went through all the usual military paper work, then stood naked in line while we waited for our physicals (quite a scene) followed by more waiting with everybody asking everyone else questions as to what did we expect would happen and when. Most everyone agreed that we would be aboard a train before nightfall headed for the Great Lakes training center somewhere in Michigan. We spent all day in this process.

Every few minutes the PA system announced that still another numbered group should report to track number so and so and climb aboard. The massive group of young men that had arrived earlier was steadily diminishing and we still hadn't been called with a track number. Finally, along about dinner time a cryptic announcement was given, "all aviation flight crew members return to your company offices immediately". We collectively breathed a sigh of relief, as we realized we could sleep at home one more night. So our group quickly rushed around getting onto subways, trains or whatever, to get out of there before the Navy changed its mind.

As I sat on the Long Island Rail Road, I pondered what would happen to me next. All I knew at that point was that I was officially in the Navy, but I didn't have a clue just what that meant except that my rank was now Aviation Chief Radioman. Some of the crew were given Lieutenant JG, if they had a college degree. The flight engineer was ranked as an Aviation Chief Mechanic. The skippers were either Lt. or Lt. Commander, if they had Navy time.

The Navy had already delivered several of their sea planes to PAA and I was checked out right away because of my high seniority. That's how I got to stay home waiting for Ken to arrive. For my own reference the U. S. Navy amphibian aircraft I was checked out on were N7083, N7086 and N7087.

I believe I was one of the first to check out on the newly delivered Navy planes. Their radio gear and Loran were great. So I got to fly around and around New England while a group of pilots checked out on the Navy PB2Y3 Consolidated Coronado four engined amphibian. During these flights Captain Harold Gray checked out Captains Gulbransen and Delima. The FROs I checked out included DR, SM, FM AND GC all newly trained FROs who aren't on my old list.

Just before my first official flight for the Navy, I had been issued khaki and olive drab uniforms, that at a distance looked like a Naval uniform but they were slightly different. I liked the olive drab one the best.

On Sept 12, 1943, we left La Guardia Bay aboard the N7087 with Capt. Mitchell bound for Fort de France via Bermuda and returned via San Juan and Bermuda. Those babies were extremely noisy as there was no sound proofing and poor heating. But the radio gear was certainly better than we had on the Clippers. It also had advanced navigational equipment such as LORAN, Long range navigation. Loran would give very accurate position fixes in a few minutes with no difficult calculations and no learning curve. Anyone could learn to use the system in minutes. The r/t flight time was 25:15 minutes.

We carried a load of mysterious crates, boxes and packages

that no one took time to say what the stuff was. Even the Navy personnel were of course close mouthed about who they were or where they were headed. Needless to say, we were kind of curious but essentially found out nothing. Do any of you remember the war saying "Loose lips sinks ships"? That is what everyone was trying not to do. Name, rank and serial number was supposed to be the extent of what they would say about themselves. Those Navy planes were all painted dull sea gray as were PAA 's nine Boeing B-314s.

The Boeing interior had also drastically been changed. The berths, some flooring and other unnecessary or luxury passenger comforts were removed to make space for more cargo and the age of shuttling had begun. Joe Hart one of the skippers crossed the Atlantic 12 times in 13 days. I commonly had five round trips across the South Atlantic between Natal and Fish Lake, plus a couple of trips to Lisbon from Fish Lake all in 30 days.

Essentially we carried priority passengers and cargo on both the B-314 and the PB2Y3s. The only real difference was that on the Navy flights, we often went into Naval bases some of which were supposed to be real secret especially Lough Neigh in northwest Ireland where we flew military VIPs into late at night. Also on the South Atlantic flights we'd stop at a Navy base, Port Lyautey in Morocco.

We flew Admirals, Generals, Kings and Queens like King George of Greece and Queen Wilhelmina of the Netherlands, lots of USO groups including film stars such as Bob Hope, Francis Langford, Jerry Colonna, Martha Raye and Carmen Miranda. I was on board when we took that particular group to North Africa in 1943 via the South Atlantic and into Fish Lake where connections were made with Army flights.

One night flight across the mid Atlantic we had Clare Booth Luce as a passenger. She was the writer and wife of the Time Life publisher. The couple of times I passed her bunk in the middle of the night I could hear the click, click of her typewriter behind the night curtains. She wrote about her flight "Fifty years from now, people will look back on a Clipper flight of today as the most romantic voyage of history"

And I agreed with her completely. Despite the stress, sweat, sleepiness and fear there was a romance about each flight. It seems a bit hard to explain to those who had not experienced it. But it was most always fun too. Each closely knit crew were

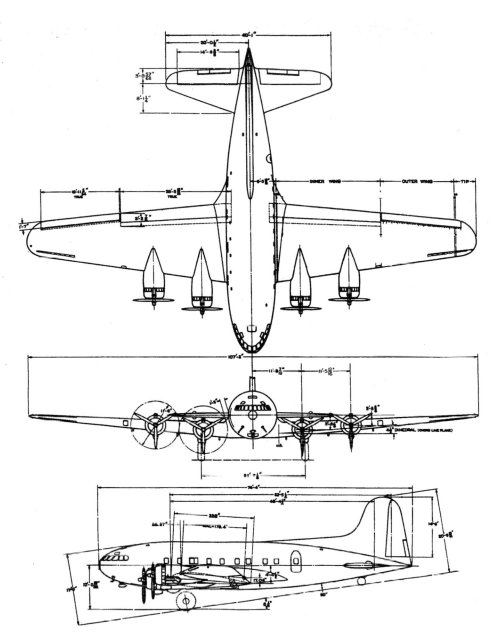

Three View of Boeing 307

all professionals in their own field but we all enjoyed a joke or two to lighten up a tiring long flight.

Sometime during the summer of 1943 our crew had a four day layover in Lisbon waiting for the next inbound flight from New York. We had flown in from the Azores the night before. Pan Am billeted us at the former royal palace of Prince Don Carlos, son of the King of Portugal. It had been renamed the Aviz Hotel. It was truly a spectacularly furnished place on the beautiful broad Aveneda Liberdade, in downtown Lisbon. .

It must have been noon when several of us had finally risen. We were all hungry so agreed to get coffee and a sandwich at one of the many lovely sidewalk cafes in the middle of the wide and busy Aveneda. The downtown Lisbon area had gorgeous flower gardens that bloomed most of the year. It was sunny and romantic, as we sat and absorbed the warm sunshine. After ordering we slid into our usual custom of girl watching.

At lunchtime these broad Avenedas with their artistic mosaic sidewalks, were crowded with pretty senoritas slowly sauntering past us. As they passed, some would give us sly smiles others a big grin. They knew we young Americans were watching their every movement. Some had real bouncy steps.

I sat with Jake our Flight Engineer. He had a slight hazy stare that began to form as a particularly attractive young lady glided past. We both looked at each other and began nodding our heads and grinning. We enthusiastically agreed that she was stunning. Her physical attributes rang our bells.

Now Jake was one of those men who liked technical things especially math. He'd sit in front of the Flight Engineer's instrument panel of gauges and switches and doodle with numbers. He designed formulas to solve his flight problems. He carried a small plastic pocket slide rule (before computers) to work out a problem. We watched him solve the pounds of fuel remaining on board. This was always the question. Did we have enough fuel to our destination plus one hour to spare. I knew an idea was forming as we sipped the great strong coffee. He whipped out his slide rule and wet his stubby pencil tip with his tongue. He put down some numbers on a paper napkin.

He suggested we get serious about rating the swarms of young lovelies passing us. So we decided we'd try rating them by the mammary movement (MM) or M2. It would be a beat system calculated on each two steps they took. Then we began to add other factors because it seemed more complicated then we first thought.

Jake did a series of calculations on mass versus diameter versus density and time. Then he tried to estimate total volume that would be needed to fill say a 36B cup bra and on to a 38D cup. After filling a couple of pages in his pocket note book with numbers, he decided that a 36C could be the norm. Here's how he figured it out. The breast would bounce upward on the first step and immediately drop down. On the next step, the other half of the cycle would be completed, identical to the first step. This kind of bouncy breast movement, he avered, would be rated as a two beater.

We two eager young 28 year old male chauvinist pigs (MCP) with nothing more important to do at that moment tried out the system. We very soon found out that there were many variables that we'd not taken into consideration. For instance:

A. Length of stride.
B. Steps per minute ie casual, moderate or in a big hurry.
C. Body weight and height.
D. Bra and cup size.
E. Bra material: durable cotton, sheer netting or neither.
F. Blouse material, button location and fit.

Jake and I dedicated over an hour on this fascinating session until the crowds began to thin. Our initial findings were that the absolutely best and most sensational rating was a 2 1/2 beater. Those topped the list and we saw several during this first test observation.

This silly pastime of ours seemed to catch on quickly by word of mouth. It wasn't long before other Lisbon layover crews were sitting having a leisure lunch in their own cafe observation posts as they busily eyeballed the busty beauties as they passed.

We soon ran into a problem on some of our later observation sessions. And we weren't able to make an accurate rating on one particular type of lovely lady. If we saw she was braless and in a hurry our rating system went out the window. The multiple movements of the mammary mass messed our minds and confused our senses. We just had to rate those as 2-1/2 plus!

So this commentary is a moments glance into old time flight crew history as to how we exhausted flyboys spent time resting and recreating R and R. Many other flyboys were much more active as you may have read about in the past. Those more romantic escapades between a few handsome single. Captains and Pan Am's delightful Stewardesses. They were legend but that's not my story here.

By present day 1990's standards of feminine ethics, we old MCP's were looking at those lovely Lisbon ladies as sex objects. I now know that was wrong and I apologize to the modern feminist for my bold and thoughtless statements of yore, "them were the facts Ms". I've tried to modify my present day behavior and have tried not to play that game any more. (At least I don't say the ratings out loud any more.)

Chapter 22

PAA Flies FDR to Casablanca

Probably what later became a very well known and famous flight started out in early 1943 as an ultra secret flight which was designated as special mission #71.

The Navy secretly arranged with the New York Atlantic Division manager Leslie for two B-314s to be in Miami with the usual double crew. When the first Boeing docked at Dinner Key in Miami, they were told to standby for a passenger "Mr. Jones" and leave immediately, as soon as he was on board.

The mysterious passenger "Mr. Jones" fully cloaked and in a wheel chair was lifted aboard, followed by a small group that appeared to be carefully protecting the wheel chaired passenger. The crew immediately recognized their passenger as President Roosevelt. They were shocked and surprised as no

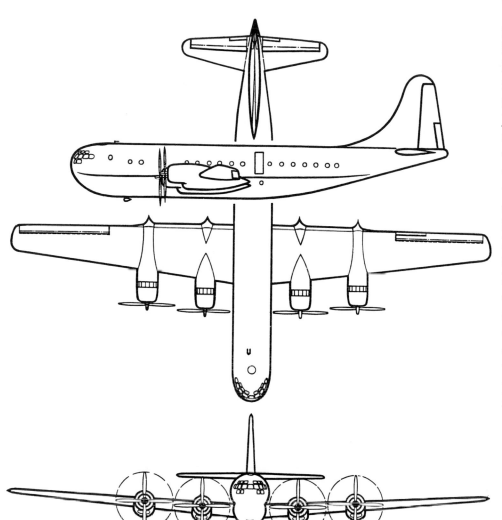

Three View of Boeing 377 Stratocruiser

he was initiated into the "Short Snorters Club".

A bit of personal background on this famous flight. For once my memory is a bit fuzzy on these details but I thought I had been assigned to the second, decoy flight that was to takeoff from Miami 30 minutes ahead of the plane that "Mr. Jones" was on. At the last minute, I was replaced by Stan Call and I never knew why. The reason I have mentioned this was that I had been the acting Chief FRO when Chief Harry Drake was needed elsewhere. So I had been privy to the very briefest of details on this hush-hush trip . My best guess on why my memory seems fuzzy was that probably Division Manager Leslie had told me to handle the communications details for the two flights, take care of them and then destroy anything written and forget all the rest. Someone above me may have shifted the whole flight crew at the last minute to prevent any possible leaks about the flight. Who knows?

Chapter 23

Whitaker Remembered Atlantic Flying

one had been told about this especially important VIP. Leslie had told no one, not even Trippe.

What was later reported, Capt. Cone had been handed a sealed envelope when he left La Guardia, N. Y. and told to open it only after passengers had been boarded in Miami. On opening the envelope, it confirmed that FDR was indeed aboard, and that they were to fly him to Fishermans Lake. He'd then be driven a few miles to the Monrovia airport where the Army Air Force would transport him to Casablanca for a conference with Prime Minister Churchill and Stalin.

On FDR's return flight the Clipper met him at Fishermans Lake. On that night flight somewhere over the South Atlantic, he celebrated his 61st birthday with a cake decorated by one of the stewards. According to Harry Hopkins, FDR enjoyed his flight tremendously as it was the first time he had been able to fly since taking office. When the flight crossed the equator

George Whitaker is still another friend and ex PAA FRO. He has kindly sent me a few memories that he said I could use. I'm quoting George here.

"In May 1944, I was a second FRO on a Boeing B-314A, Clipper, the most beautiful plane ever built. We had just landed on the Tagus River at Lisbon, Portugal. PAA housed the flight crew at the Palacio Hotel in Estoril, about 20 miles outside of Lisbon. This was a super deluxe hotel that catered to the wealthy of Europe prior to WWII. Apparently PAA wanted their crews to stay at the best. We lived like kings. The hotel faced a street that led to a casino. In front of the casino was a large flower garden that flowed several blocks to a boulevard that overlooked the Atlantic Ocean. One night I accompanied a group from the crew to the casino. The usual gambling

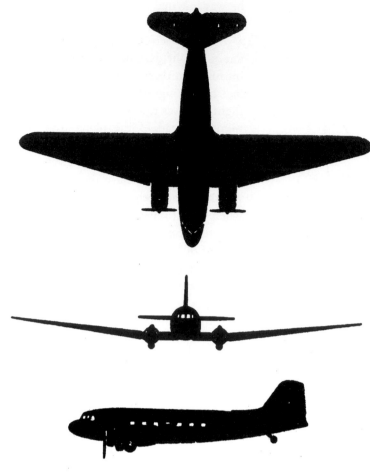

Three View of Douglas DC-3

devices of roulette and cards were in evidence but no slot machines. Suddenly a chill of apprehension came over me as I saw among the crowd of people, the enemy. This was in the middle of WWII and to see Germans and Japanese at the tables was a shock. My patriotic blood was flowing fast. Portugal as a neutral, made Lisbon haven for agents of every political stripe. Some PAA crew members had become involved in harassing the enemy but not that night."

"The next day we flew down the west coast of Africa to Liberia then across the South Atlantic to Natal, Brazil. On our return trip to Lisbon, D-Day 1944 occurred. Again in Estoril I attended the casino. To me the faces of the Germans and Japanese had lost the carefree but haughty look that I had seen before. Now they were sullen and somber as if D-Day had forecast their doom. I shall never forget the feeling of being in the midst of the enemy and unable to do anything about it".

George's second experience is centered around Lisbon also. "During the war, one was allowed to leave and return to the USA with a maximum of $50. in cash but unlimited travelers checks. The money changers in Lisbon would sell two USA dollars for one dollar in a travelers check. These dollars had gold seals on them as they were usually issued to the service men. A unique opportunity presented itself to me. I could have taken $1,000. in travellers checks from home and purchased $2,000. in cash in Lisbon. Then I could fly to Natal,

Brazil. At the Army PX, I could buy a money order to myself and mail it home. I never took advantage of this opportunity as I thought this was a way the enemy laundered the money they had taken from our service people. Though I never knew of anyone who participated in such a scheme, I'm sure I was not the only one who thought of it". He was right.

Another experience George mentioned follows: "The third event happened between Lisbon and Foynes, Ireland. Our flight plan took the Boeing B-314A Clipper along the coasts of Portugal and Spain. It was in this area that a plane similar to ours was shot down by the Germans who were based in France. Through the foreign intrigue in Lisbon, they knew a VIP was on board that flight and thought it was Prime Minister Churchill. Instead it was the movie star, Leslie Howard, who was killed".

"It was in this area that our plane suddenly encountered severe weather conditions. At an altitude of over 10,000 feet, ice began to form on the aircraft. The two outboard engines lost power and stopped functioning. With only two engines operating the plane began to descend rapidly. As the FRO on duty, the Captain told me to send a message to Lisbon that we are returning, due to engine failure. I sent the message also giving our location. To reduce the weight of the aircraft, the flight engineer began to 'dump' fuel into the air. While the gas was being released, Captain Winston, was sitting in the cockpit saying 'We will hit in 20 seconds, we will hit the water in 15 seconds'. . ."

"But we didn't! Just enough fuel had been dumped to lighten the weight of the aircraft enough to maintain altitude of a few hundred feet. So for the next 4-1/2 hours we limped back to Lisbon. We skimmed over the waves sometimes at 500 feet and sometimes all the way up to 2,000 feet then we'd drop back down again a few feet above the waves. Finally we landed safely."

"Talking to the pilots afterwards, they said they could look up and see the waves. The mechanics at Lisbon said they found salt spray in the engine nacelles of the defective engines. We definitely were very low and yet no one was hurt. If the plane had hit the ocean in that storm none would have survived. I always said the Lord had other things for me to do, such as get married to Stella and have two sons, Warren and Dwight."

One last quote from George is where he is again talking about Lisbon. I think almost all the flight crews loved that city. I know I sure did.

"PAA did provide the best accommodations for the crews in Lisbon during the war. I remember the Aviz Hotel that usually housed royalty. Silk sheets covered the beds. The bathtub was on a dais that had marble steps on three sides and a large mirror at the head. The big event of the day was collecting the 20 escudos, the company gave us for tipping. One dollar equaled 20 escudos then. We would walk to colonnade mall and get our shoes shined". George and Stella live a few hours away, in New Jersey.

Chapter 24

A B314 Engine Change in Primitive Bolama-PAA Hired Jeanne Elise as Stewardess

One of my last flights on a Boeing B-314 was a Mid Atlantic circle trip starting from New York to Lisbon and on south to Bolama where we ran into real trouble. A week on that tiny island was some experience.

It happened like this. As we were an hour or so out of Bolama, we heard a terrible noise from number three engine and the oil pressure dropped to zero. The Flight Engineer quickly shut the engine down and we made a normal approach and landing at Bolama.

After hours of careful inspection, the Flight Engineers determined that we had blown a cylinder along with other problems. The consensus was that we would have to wait there while New York sent in a special flight with a replacement engine, cranes and maintenance help.

Now I'll tell you the Bolama base radio operator was on continuous duty for 24 hours because he found himself a most popular man with his two way radio communications gear. We had to send dozens of messages back and forth between maintenance in New York and our Flight Engineers who hung out in the radio shack either sending or receiving messages. All of this was taking place on the lightly populated little tiny island of Bolama, in the Atlantic, with few tools and no cranes to handle a ton of engine. I'm trying to recall who was stationed there then: either Ralph Petersen or Don Oliva.

The passengers had to be offloaded and waited two days until the next south bound flight came along to pick them up and take them on to New York via Fish Lake and Natal. Because of the heat, the whole crew was stripped to the waist while we helped the two engineers slowly take the engine apart and prepare for the spare engine to arrive.

I'm guessing but I would think an aircraft engine with its three bladed prop attached would weigh 1,500 lbs.. So the engineers arranged for a local carpenter to build a floating barge affair that could be used to mount the engine crane and block and tackle that was arriving with the spare engine. It seems as if the engineers made a lot of makeshift and ingenious rigs so they could work on the engine. They had to work inside

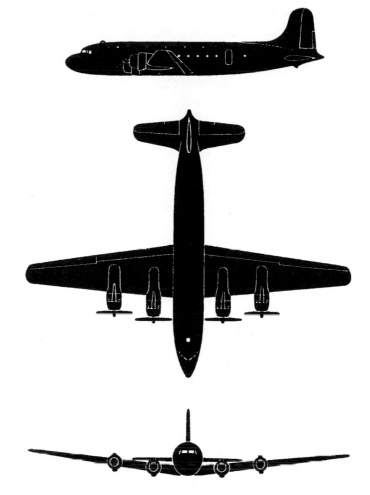

Three View of Douglas DC-4

the engine catwalk in the boiling heat or stand 15 feet above the water where we were docked. I don't know how many tools were dropped overboard into the bay, along with some healthy swearing, before a canvas drop cloth sling was tied beneath the wing.

The bottom line is, along with collective efforts of the crew but especially the two Flight Engineers, the damaged engine was removed and replaced with a new one. There was much struggling, grunting, shouted commands, many skinned knuckles, banged heads, sweaty bodies, coke and beer drunk, before this was done. The engine nuts, bolts, fuel and oil line connections, spark plug harnesses and many dozens of things were checked and inspected twice. The tense moment came when we were ready to start the engine. And it did start, first with a few backfiring bangs and then into a satisfying roar, finally. A pleasant noise indeed. Oil pressure was up, engine head temperatures okay and it ran for half an hour before everything was declared AOK. We took a half hour local test flight before we headed back to New York empty via Dakar, Belem, San Juan and North Beach.

I want to mention that Pan American began hiring young women as Stewardesses. In fact, the company hired Dear Flo's sister Jeanne Elise Rodgers in Miami in the summer of 1943. LIFE magazine carried an interview with Jeanne as being one of the first Stewardesses to be hired by Pan Am. They described her qualities as fascinating and a beautiful young woman, with personality and poise, who spoke Spanish and French. The article went on to describe the glamour and excitement of flying to foreign places.

After six weeks of training in Coconut Grove, Jeanne began her flights to San Juan. The Puerto Rican people had even back then, begun a steady migration to Miami. So PAAs flights from San Juan always flew into Miami fully loaded. She said it seemed to her that many of her passengers were frightened to fly and immediately became air sick. It was extremely difficult to clean up the mess while trying to serve an attractive meal at the same time. So flying wasn't always glamorous for all the crew.

When I talked with Jeanne last week, she reminded me of several things. I asked her what was one of her favorite stories about being a Flight Attendant. Her instant reply was "I almost spilled coffee on the Captain's lap! But I married him later."

She told me it happened on her first flight out of Miami Municipal Airport when they were headed for Cristobal, Panama. I gather she was so excited to be on her initial flight and serving coffee to a handsome Skipper that sparks flew between them. The Captain's name was Mike Brake, a handsome hunk who became my brother in law.

It appeared to be a mutual attraction, as a romance developed quickly between Jeanne and Mike. If I recall correctly, they were married fairly soon after they met. I believe they had to keep it a secret, as Stewardesses were not allowed to fly and be married too. What a ridiculous rule that was.

Throughout the rest of 1943, I flew hundreds of hours aboard the Coronado PB2Y3 Navy flying boats dozens of times across the South Atlantic. We made new ports of call at British, Dutch and other neutral ports. For example we began flying between Natal and Bathurst, British Guinea; Port Lyautey, Morocco; Dakar, Senegal; and Paramaribo, Suriname; on the Northern coast of South America.

Rubber tires, tires and more tires. We must have carried thousands or even a million or more tires everywhere to keep the thousands of Jeeps running. Those Naval flights went via the South Atlantic to various non-PAA ports in NW Africa.

More tires. Capt. Gray made a famous special missions trip from New York to Calcutta on the Boeing B314, carrying aircraft spare parts including hundreds of Jeep tires and tracer ammunition for the Flying Tigers and the Royal Air Force in Burma. Skipper Gray's Clipper completed the 29,801 mile round trip in 207 hours, making a new record and blazing an aerial trail that later proved invaluable to Air Transport Command (ATC) supply lines to the Tigers and the Far East.

I suspect a whole book could be written about all the famous world leaders and near famous who were carried aboard the Clippers to everywhere in the world. In addition, there was a lot more war materials carried than any one of us wanted to know about. We would have been even more frightened about some of the flights, if we had known. The crews were too involved in doing a good job and buried any real concerns about where we were flying to or what we had on board.

Chapter 25

Willmott's and Liese's Flight Memories, My Navy Trips

John Willmott was best man at my wedding to Florence. He had flown as PAA FRO in Miami and later in the Atlantic division for a short time. He went on to get his commercial pilot's license and flew for Pan Am. Then for a while he was with a secret U. S. government-PAA airline called Atlantic Airways Ltd. (AA) ferrying planes everywhere. I think this was before we got into the war. Later AA was renamed PAA Air Ferries.

I visited John and his wife Joan in Dorset, Vermont. very recently. He has always been a fine photographer and took thousands of photos on his many flights. I've borrowed a few to add to my memoirs. Of course we had to relive some of our flights. I'll quote Johnny along with a minilove story.

"When I first saw her she was floating sun soaked in the blue-green waters of Biscayne Bay. She looked slinky-lean, with bumps, bends and curves in all the right places. Small wavelets caressed her from head to foot as she rose and fell sensuously on a slight swell coming through the inlet from the open sea."

"I am not one to fall in love at first sight but, oh my gosh, Nan was beautiful-almost beyond anything I'd seen lately. I think I've always had an affinity for water creatures be they fish, fowl, men, women or machines. As I stood watching I thought of Nan and me visiting exotic, far away places; of fun in the sun, of starlit skies, and of resting in the shade under breeze ruffled palms as surf pounds on a golden sandy beach extending from here to the horizon."

"My reverie was broken by Bill's sharp command, "come on John, let's get our gear aboard and fly her". Nan was a Consolidated twin engined PBY5A long range patrol bomber, mostly used by the Navies of the world, for patrol over open ocean, search and rescue, and in anti-submarine searches and bombing.

"Bill Cleveland was one of a rather rare breed of old time pilots experienced as flying boat and landplane captains He and several other experienced seaplane pilots had come to Atlantic Airways Limited when it became known we would be ferrying seaplanes in addition to the various military and civilian landplanes we had already flown over the South Atlantic to Africa, the Mideast and beyond, during the past year, since May, 1941. There were only a few qualified seaplane pilots then, free to take a job ferrying. There were a few recently out of the Navy but most were employed by international airlines such as Pan American Airways or British Overseas Airlines and Lufthansa.. Some others came from jobs flying for wealthy private or corporate plane owners. Bill had been a corporate pilot after his Navy tour. Bud had been flying a twin engine Grumman flying boat for the Vanderbilt family on Long Island. Some had flown seaplanes as bush pilots in Alaska and Canada while others had flown all over the world for oil exploration teams. All in all we were a motley crew of adventurers, soldiers of fortune, gentlemen and rogues-not necessarily in that order".

"When I refer to my pilot's log book, I can take a flight of fancy -fond remembrance-way back and relive an actual flight to some far away romantic place sharing adventures with friends and colleagues as we helped make aviation history."

"In 1944, I was still on crew rest at my converted boathouse home on Bay Avenue, Huntington, Long Island. I had returned on May 22, from an 18 day trip to a Navy base at Port Lyautey, near Casablanca, Morocco. No, it was not a slow boat to Africa but I was a junior birdman and chief bowline catcher on a USN Consolidated Coronado PB2Y3 4 engine flying boat. The route was North Beach marine terminal (La Guardia) to San Juan, Port of Spain, Belem, Natal, Dakar to Casablanca. The return trip reversed the routing and I arrived back home on Navy aircraft no.. 7077, trip no.. 334. Since it was warm weather, I presume I used my sailboat anchored out front and or went fishing, which I often did before a breakfast of 4 or 5 small young flounders for breakfast. Delicious!"

"About the time the invasion at Normandy was announced on the 6th of June, I was informed that I would crew a special flight across the North Atlantic to Northern Ireland with supplies for the invasion. On June 8th, we departed on Navy Coronado PB2Y3 no.. 7100, trip no.. 363 from North Beach for Botwood on the North coast of Newfoundland taking 6.5 hours. From Botwood, it was to Lough Neigh, a large inland lake about 15 miles west of Belfast. The flight time was 11.3 hours. Arriving over the beacon shortly after dawn, there was no lake or land visible due to a low fog. A direction finder approach using the ADF, was made with a timed 200 foot a minute descent letdown from overhead the beacon, to a blind

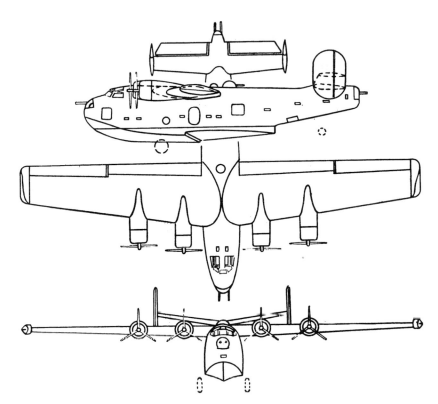

Three View Consolidated PB2Y3 as flown by Pan Am crews

splashdown. It was totally a blind landing in dense fog."

"As captain of the anchor, I dropped it overboard and then we took turns blowing into the foghorn. Really! Shortly after that, we heard voices and a weird apparition ghosted toward us out of the fog. It was a fishing boat-the largest rowing boat I'd ever seen-and it was manned by 5 or 6 men looking like elves, gnomes or old wrinkled farmers in rubber boots and strange hats. Take your pick. It took forever- perhaps 30 minutes for the Navy launch to show up. He was lost! Eventually it towed us to dockside."

"The return trip of the Coronado 7100, took 17.2 hours. I say again, 17.2 hours nonstop against headwinds sometimes flying barely above the ocean surface, to arrive at Botwood; thence another 6.3 hours to North Beach, a total of 23.5 hours."

"What makes this interesting to the young, the new age pilots and modern travellers is that other than the Pan Am Boeing B-314 Clippers, there were no large landplanes and runways for them, available for transocean flying at that time. Also, compare the flight time of 23.5 hours with the time from London to New York of 6.5 hours by modern jet. It was the war and its B17 and Liberator bombers which brought long runways and ushered in the new era of landplanes. For many years after the war an argument persisted between using flying boats on unlimited water or landplanes on very expensive long concrete. I am glad I helped pioneer world travel and have many very happy memories of places and doing things, romances and good friends. I also lost two friends and roommates from early Pan Am at Dinner Key, Miami. One died fly-

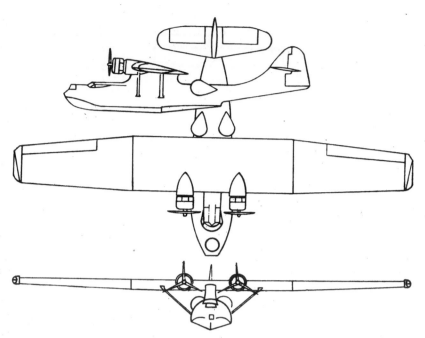

Three View of Consolidated PBY5A as flown by Pan Am crews

ing a B25 Mitchell bomber overseas and the other died training Navigators in Miami on a Catalina PBY flying boat."

"While writing this 50 years later, I am thankful for every dawn, every sunset, every lilac perfumed springtime."

Thanks Johnny for those memories. You proved once more the value of having good DF equipment on board and a FRO who knew how to use it, otherwise you might have become a statistic. and I echo your current feeling too, about being thankful!

Along with the photos I borrowed from Johnny, I'd copied a couple of pages from his ferry pilot log book. I quote him: "My epic odyssey (as a Ferry Pilot) began Dec. 28, 1941 on a Catalina, PBY, Nan 71, from Miami to Surabaja, Java for the Royal Dutch Navy and my return by Empire flying boat to Pakistan from whence I returned by military C47 (DC-3) to Africa, thence to be picked up by Pan Am Boeing B-314 Clipper and returned to New York, returning to Miami by domestic airline".

Charles Liese, another Pan Am FRO, who I recently caught up with also, sent me a few incidents he describes. "On a flight from Natal to New York on the B-314 we landed at Bermuda. We learned that North Beach was closed due to weather minimums and we'd be going to Norfolk, Virginia, seaplane base. So after takeoff from Bermuda, it was my turn for bunk time. We climbed to altitude and I was quite comfortable with the drone of the engines when all of a sudden the engine power was cut and the aircraft started descending fast. Well, let me tell you, in a microsecond I found myself on the flight deck. `What's happening?` `Oh nothing` I was told, `we're picking up a little ice and just wanted to get down in a hurry!` I was too young to have a heart attack."

"One night we were flying a DC-4 into Santa Maria, Azores at 8,000 feet. We could see Horta, the old seaplane base, so I

put my head through the curtain and asked the pilots if they could see Pico. What's Pico, was the question. I told them its an 8,000 foot mountain. They laughed and said, there aren't any mountains out here in the ocean. Let me see and into the cockpit I went. As I looked and pointed you could see Pico and we were headed right for the top. As I moved out of the cockpit, I could feel the plane climbing. I figured I'd earned my pay that day, or was it just fate."

"Departing Gander, in a L049 Connie and climbed to 16,000 feet bound for La Guardia. We knew the winds were strong at this altitude but we were above the bad weather. After taking many good radio bearings and being surprised how strong they were, we figured out that in one hour we had made only 90 miles! In other words, the headwind was 160 MPH"

"On another Connie flight we took off from La Guardia to Heathrow direct, on a daylight crossing. As we neared the coast of the UK and close to France, the bearings I took were all bad or so I thought. The cockpit saw a shore light or beacon that might have been on the coast of France. At the time I called London on an emergency VHF frequency and obtained a course to fly to reach Heathrow and we needed it. It sure would have made lots of paper work had we landed in Paris!!!"

"On a clear night flight from Johannesburg, South Africa to Leopoldville, Belgian Congo, the Connie was making good time. Everything was okay thought the pilot/navigator, until the cockpit looked down and in the moonlight saw nothing but water. It was the South Atlantic! The navigator had applied the magnetic variation the wrong way (subtracting instead of adding) which gave a resultant course error of 40 degrees. They reworked the navigation and flew up the coast. Pappy Martin was the FRO and he obtained bearings from a marine coastal station giving good cross bearings. The Captain figured he could always ditch on the beach if necessary. But luck or fate was with them and they made it".

"After the end of World War II, I was on the La Guardia to London leg of the inaugural flight to Vienna. During the crossing, Juan Trippe came up into the cockpit, introduced himself and asked about communications. When I think today, how few people realize when they ride on a Boeing 747, that Juan Trippe had so much to do with its design. His was the first order for 25 Boeing 747s. Delivery of the whole fleet would occur before anyone else could get one plane." Thanks lots Charlie. He and his wife Ella live in Barre, Vermont.

For the next two years, 1944 and 1945, I spent a great deal of time flying the Navy flying boats. I crisscrossed the North,

Mid and South Atlantic many dozens of times. We would fly from Botwood, Newfoundland to Lough Neigh near Belfast, Ireland, then south to Port Lyautey in Morocco. We'd complete the trip by flying directly from Port Lyautey to Belem then San Juan, Bermuda and North Beach. Somewhere along about mid 1946, the company gave me a certificate stating I had crossed the Atlantic 100 times. They even gave me a publicity photo of me on the Connie which appears in these pages.

The only time we were ever shot at was on a night flight from Fish Lake to Natal. We were flying west between 500 and 1000 feet to make the best speed against the head winds. Suddenly we saw bright white tracers directly ahead. The Skipper quickly dropped a wing and made a steep turn to avoid getting hit and we passed over whatever was shooting at us. It had to have been a German sub that had surfaced to charge its batteries. Regularly we were given written reports of sub sightings by other flights. We did the same.

Chapter 26

Death of my Friend Oscar Olsen aboard China Clipper

The famous China Clipper, Martin M-130, NC14716 had been sent to the Eastern Division in 1943. Originating out of Miami, it was flying war supplies and special VIP's across Africa and on to the Middle East. I've quoted from Barry Taylor's book "Pan American's Ocean Clippers".

This particular flight I'm quoting here left Miami on Jan. 8, 1945, headed for Allied controlled Leopoldville, Belgian Congo with war supplies. "The China Clipper approached Port of Spain, Trinidad, on a direct night flight from Miami. There were 30 souls aboard Flight 161 that night: 18 passengers and 12 crew members, with Captain Cyril Gayette at the controls. The weather was fine, in fact, beautiful, with a bright moon and few clouds. Approaching Port of Spain, Gayette decided to change seats with Captain Leonard Cramer, who was acting as first officer-a common occurrence on long distance flights-to give Cramer some practice in night landings. Cramer would make the landing from the left seat".

"Flight 161 received instructions from Pan American-Miami at 7:30 PM to contact Port of Spain for the weather. The Martin flying boat was number one to land in the Corcorite area at 9 PM, an anchorage about 10 miles off the Trinidad coast. Crossing the North coast of the island, the China Clipper's altitude was 4,000 feet, still too high to land on a final approach, so Cramer started a 360 degree turn to the left to come around again. But there were hills in that direction. Gayette told Cramer to make his turn to the right instead."

"Final approach placed the aircraft three miles from the number one light at the anchorage at approximately 1,000 feet The rate of descent was 600 feet per minute at 105 knots. The aircraft was right on course. 800 feet above the water, rate of descent was 300 feet per minute and speed was 100 knots. There was a light haze at around 400 feet but this was of little consequence. The Clipper was approximately 1/2 mile from the first anchorage light. The huge ship cast a giant shadow on the water, silvery in the moonlight, 250 feet, 100 knots."

"Suddenly, there was a terrific crash. Captain Leonaard Cramer would later describe it as `a shearing noise followed by a sudden lurch.`"

"The Martin Clipper came to a sudden stop, the hull broken in two; water poured into the cabin, and a major part of the aircraft sank immediately. 16 passengers and 9 crew members died".

"The official investigation gave the probable cause of the crash as the pilot's `failure to realize his proximity to the water and to correct his altitude for a normal landing and lack of adequate supervision by the captain during the landing, resulting in excessive landing speed in a nose down attitude`. No mention was made of the M-130 hitting an unidentified object on the water, although unofficial versions of the accident frequently say the China Clipper hit something, such as a small boat".

"Flight Engineer John Morse, who survived the accident, probably gave the most damaging testimony, said in part . . ."

"The string of landing lights were distinctly visible, strung out in approximately an east-west direction, and I noticed one launch in its proper position. I could see ripples on the surface of the water, and it seemed odd to me that the surface of the water and the top surface of the sea wing seemed parallel, so I concluded we were in a gliding position. Normally, at that height above the water the upper surface of the hydrostabilizer would have been pointing at an up-angle of approximately 15 degrees with the surface of the water. I could see no light whatsoever except that given by the left landing light. When I realized the imminence of our landing, I tightened my safety belt and at that instant, as far as I can remember, we touched the water . . ."

"And so the China Clipper met the same fate as the other two Martin M-130s - the aircraft that had probably done more to stimulate aircraft development and public acceptance (in the Pacific) than any others of their age. Strangely, the death of the China Clipper, with so much else happening in the world at that time, went almost unnoticed by the public. Perhaps it was just as well, better to remember the giant Clipper as she was in her heyday, the romantic lead in one of the best shows on earth."

She had been a star ten years earlier when, for the first time, she opened air travel from San Francisco, over the wide Pacific to all of the Orient.

The tremendously sad note I've left until last. My special friends and roommates Oscar Olson and Tom Fleming, both died in that crash. I hadn't heard about it for many days afterward. I was stunned and emotionally hung up. I left on a flight to Belem shortly after hearing about his death. I buried my emotions somehow. That seemed to be what we crew members did when we heard this kind of news. I had not stayed in touch with Oscar as he was in a different division and our paths didn't cross. His death touched me deeply, when I let myself think about it. It was so close to home. God be with them both.

Chapter 27
Lockheed L049 Connie Delivery, Landplane Conversion, Miami Seaplane Base Closed

It was Jan. 1946, that we got word that Pan Am was getting the sleek new high speed, pressurized four engined Lockheed L049 Constellation, nicknamed the Connie. I got myself assigned to pick up that new baby at the Lockheed plant at Burbank.

The three man crew of Captain, copilot and me, flew out to Burbank, to wait for what was supposed to be an immediate delivery. Each morning at 8 AM, one of us would check in with Lockheed and ask if it was ready. And each morning they would say the same thing, "No, not today". This went on for six whole weeks.

Luckily for me, my brother Paul lived very close to the Lockheed Burbank plant, so I got to stay with him. I couldn't stand waiting around and not do something constructive all day. (My Puritan ethics?) So I talked myself into a job at the busy corner gas station pumping gas and oil changes. For some reason the boss liked me and assigned me to work on Hollywood actress Ann Sheridan's white convertible Packard. That car was one of her pets. She brought it in weekly, to be gassed, washed and polished. I got to talk with her a little bit, got a big kick out of that. The boss paid me in cash. I've forgotten how much but I really didn't care, it was fun and besides I was getting per diem along with my regular salary. I

was even saving money!

Six weeks after our arrival, Feb. 1946, Lockheed said yes, the Connie was ready and we were too! The three of us met the Lockheed crew at Burbank airport. They gave us a short briefing and we took off for Las Vegas, Nevada. I was immensely impressed with all the shiny new equipment and how fast it had raced down the runway and lifted off, in what seemed to be only 15 seconds or so. Of course we had no real weight, five people and probably very little gas.

After we taxied over to one of the ramps and shut everything down, all three of us were very extensively checked out on the equipment by Lockheed representatives. We were given what seemed like a couple of hundreds pounds of operations manuals and the Skipper signed 40 different papers

At long last we were done and we officially accepted the plane for Pan American World Airways. This was the first Connie. The company got to like them so much that they finally bought a fleet of 28. This aircraft number was N88831, Clipper London. It could carry 45 passengers at 260 MPH, 3,000 miles and was pressurized. It had 15 sleeperettes.

You might wonder why had Lockheed taken us to Las Vegas to deliver the plane. Simple. It saved Pan Am from paying a California sales tax of $10,000. This was apparently a common practice of all aircraft manufacturers at that time.

On the flight to New York, we three ran continuous tests of all kinds. I ran and tested all the communications and navigation gear, transmitting on numerous frequencies and especially checking myself out on the LORAN which was an entirely new method of getting fast, accurate position fixes from almost anywhere and in any kind of weather. Spectacular.

The skipper shut off one engine and feathered the prop so it wouldn't windmill. We wanted to see at what altitude we could maintain. It performed according to specifications. Each of us gave it an AOK report.

Unfortunately, Clipper London had a very short life. After many training flights around North Beach and six months of regular flights, it crashed on landing at Shannon, Ireland. What a sad and costly expense that was. I'm drawing a blank on the reason for the crash. Twelve of the 28 Connies PAA had, crashed over a 20 year period. Not a great record.

At this same time, Douglas was delivering the four engined DC-4 to all divisions of Pan Am. Of the 84 or so that PAA ultimately flew, a few were leased from the Air Force. But essentially the ones we got were all ex-military and were rebuilt to fit PAAs commercial specifications. I had only two roundtrip flights on one, both were La Guardia to San Juan.

When I got home from delivering the first Connie to the Atlantic Division, I read in the Clipper NEWS, our company newspaper, that they had closed down Dinner Key in Miami. The article said the company wouldn't be servicing flying boats there any more. That was sad news for me and nostalgic too. Obviously, this was the signal that the era of the romantic and majestic bird of the aviation sky, the Boeing B-314, would not be around much longer. Land planes were taking

One of three Martin M130 flying boats built for Pan Am, *Philippine Clipper* is shown arriving in Hong Kong October 23, 1936. All three of these ships were destined to crash. Pan American World Airways painting by John McCoy.

over fast.

Two innovations were inaugurated on the first few flights aboard the Connie to Europe. One was in-flight movies and the second was passengers could use the telephone while in flight. Neither was a big hit.

The story on the in-flight movies was that the FRO's had to run the projector, or at least I did on two of my Connie flights. I think it was the second time I did it that I ran into a minor mess. Dinner had been served. Passengers were settling down for the long hours ahead, when we would arrive at the Shannon, Ireland airport. The cabin lights were off and the movie screen had been pulled down for use. I got the first reel loaded and lens focused and sat beside the projector to enjoy the film. The sound quality was poor as there was only a few widely spaced speakers in the overhead. It was 8 MM film only, so the picture quality was poor.

There was only one projector, so when I came to the end of the first reel, I had to quickly shut everything off and load the second reel with a flashlight. To my great dismay, I had not threaded the takeup reel properly, and all the film had run through the projector okay but was sitting in a curly pile on the isle floor. I scrambled to get the projector going again and

finally did. The rest of the reel transfers worked okay. But it was a poor performance on my part. I don't know how many passengers were watching. The inflight movie project fizzled soon after, as I suspected it would.

The company issued several memos on the use of our radiotelephone equipment for the passengers. I think we had to get FCC approval as well as learn ITT telephone company methods for connecting to the telephone company's overseas operators. I'm vague about just what had been required to make it happen. I feel it never got off the ground as I can't recall having to do anything like that for a passenger. If I did my memory is in a blocked mode.

For the rest of 1946 I made only a few Navy flights and a few more flights on the Boeing B-314. But for the most part I was assigned to the Connie L049 flights and continued to fly them all during 1947, too.

You see, when I switched from sea planes to land planes it seemed that lots of things had changed. We landed on a paved runway, not in a harbor or river. Worldwide air traffic control had been developed which offered safer air traffic handling, such as AIRINC. PAA had built hundreds of land airports worldwide that helped make night flying possible along with better airport lighting.

There were two or three times more passengers on board with an increase in Stewardesses. The aircraft speed averaged 100 MPH faster, so we got to our destinations faster. Pressurized aircraft made flights much smoother as most of the time we were above the clouds and bad weather. The communications and navigation equipment was superior in quality, range, speed of operation and accuracy. This helped assure safer flights.

Better cockpit and airport navigation equipment made possible takeoffs and landings under much lower weather minimums. Improved aircraft and instrument ground maintenance reduced flight delays and improved utilization. Gone was the close knit team feeling, because the cockpit crew dropped from 10 to 2 or 3. Gone were the long, frequent layovers. I missed that. Gone was the excitement of pioneering flights, adventure, and challenge. The technical advancement in radio and navigating gear on this new Lockheed L049 was tremendous. The transmitters had more power, 150 watts, more efficient, with 24 channels to send on.

Radiotelephone now worked effectively over 1,000 miles or more. So CW code had become less essential. The receivers were more sensitive and selective and easier to tune. There were two automatic direction finders, with one unit and associated controls handy to either pilot. The second ADF was at the FROs position. I was especially pleased with the ease and speed of getting Loran isobar readings that could be taken on a master and slave pair, when we might be a 1,000 miles from the U. S. coastline. Those could be translated quickly to an extremely accurate position fix, to navigate by. There was no need to be in clear weather as celestial sights required or the need to look up several numbers in Air Almanac and other tables with several chances for math errors. Loran required only to observe two sets of sine waves on an oscilloscope and to transfer those numbers to an appropriate numbered chart with similar numbers, to get a fix. This would only take a minute or two. Anyone could learn to use the Loran in minutes.

The hand writing was on the wall. If any of us FROs had looked ahead, we would have realized our professional skills wouldn't be needed much longer. Pioneering distant air routes and aviation communications and the "Romance of Aviation" was soon to end. Few of us knew that our demise was still three years away.

Chapter 28

East to Karachi

Now on to more adventure and new places that the Connie would take me to, half way around the world. In the spring of 1946, my first Connie flight would take me to the Mid and Far East, starting out via a familiar route, La Guardia to Lisbon direct in ten hours. We laid over for two days, the trip continued when the next inbound flight arrived. On to new places. The leg from Lisbon to Rome took 4:35 minutes where we left most of the passengers then immediately left for Damascus and arrived after another uneventful flight of 5:50 minutes. We overnighted there at a hotel whose name I can't recall.

On this trip our cockpit crew was different than the usual big B-314 crew. It was down to four. Pilot, copilot, Flight Radio Officer and Flight Engineer. Passengers on board grew as well. We left New York with 43 on board, most of them going to Rome. I think we had three Stewardesses with us.

With young women as crew members now, the cockpit crews attitude seemed to have changed some. I felt that some viewed their arrival as a mixed blessing since they were all pretty and attractive. And we always imagined ourselves a long way from home. So for all the single young bucks, temptations often arose, and they flirted outrageously.

Personally, I have always enjoyed women, 6 to 60. To me they were a joy and was what had added sparkle to my eyes whenever I had a chance to talk with them. It wasn't often unfortunately. I know some crew members used to feel it stifled the old comradery that existed with the all male big Clipper crews. I don't think it did that.

The one thing I did note though during our layover stops. It seemed to me and to most of the rest of the crew as well, that the Stewardesses were magnetically drawn to Captains. I was never really sure just what that meant. Was it because all Captains were handsome or kind of rich or the boss on board or maybe just plan nice guys? I don't think it was their uniform, as we all had the same. Ah yes, maybe it was the gold braid, the Skippers had the most: four gold stripes.

Now, Karachi was a surprise to me, compared with Calcutta. My first visit to India had been when I was the Radio Officer on board the SS Ensley City and we had docked at Calcutta in 1936. What a depressingly poor city Calcutta seemed to me. The people seemed to be poorly fed and dressed, streets exceptionally dirty, no proper sanitation and the Brahma cows wandering the streets were holy and not to be touched. It was hot! In all, my first impression of India was bad. However I admit, I did no touring and saw very little else

The arrival of the Boeing 307 Stratoliner heralded big changes as in this 1940 scene at Miami. New airports around the world made the change to land planes possible. In a few years Dinner Key and La Guardia Marine Terminal would all close and the era of Pan Am's famous flying boats would end. Pan American World Airways.

but the dock area, so what could I expect.

Karachi was remarkably different. It was cooler, much cleaner, more industrious, with the people seemingly to be healthy and reasonably well clothed and fed. There was poverty seen but it didn't seem as wide spread as Calcutta. Of course this was ten years later so the economy may have picked up in the country some.

The hotel had large comfortable rooms and high ceilings with the lovely slowly turning ceiling fans that kept things cool. There was definitely a caste system present as there seemed to be so many young men doing such menial things around the hotel. The British influence was seen everywhere. My impression of the British on their foreign assignments was that they loved to wear those starched white suits and to be waited on, asking for their scotch and soda, vodka tonic or lemon squash. I'm sure that wasn't true of all British but so it seemed to me from my hotel observation site.

Oh yes, I meant to mention that on the 2,115 mile, 8:05 minute flight into Karachi, I was told we'd pass a round the world flight of two single engined Cessnas. They were due to arrive in Karachi also. I caught up with that fact because one of the new friendly stewardesses aboard named Lois, who

came from Teterboro, New Jersey, knew one of the two pilots who was trying for the light plane world record. They had started their flight ten days earlier from Teterboro airport.

Lois had been closely following the progress of these two Cessnas. They were supposed to be in Karachi when we got there. I listened for them on the aircraft frequencies. Sure enough 40 minutes out of Karachi I overheard two Americans chatting about where they thought they were. I think we were very close to them but our altitude was 22,000 feet and they told me they were at 2,000 feet. We kept a close lookout but never did see them. I called them on the radiophone and told them that we where a Pan Am Clipper and our ETA Karachi was 37 minutes from then. I also said I had a stewardess on board who thought she knew them. She wanted to say hello, and to meet them at the airport. They said sure that would be great. When I asked them what their ETA was, they replied, "We don't know where we are, somewhere over the muddy Indian Ocean but we sure are making great time. Maybe we'll be there in an hour or so". Our crew got a big kick out of their imprecise comments. Their flight was not being run quite so professionally as ours. But in all fairness to them we had Loran and other sophisticated equipment that helped us. We said we would wait for them at the airport. When they arrived, Lois and I were still waiting. She was so excited to met someone from her home town, half way around the world. It was fun to meet them but I left shortly after to get some bunk time.

My return flight from Karachi was uneventful. All I knew was that I was exhausted from the flight when I got back home. I know when we flew the long B-314 flights Lisbon-New York with double crews, that took 22 or 23 hours, I'd be exhausted too. My family would wonder how I could sleep 24 hours, around the clock. But now on the Connies, I was kind of expecting it to be easier. For some reason it wasn't. The longest flights were usually only ten hours or so, with no relief. I guess that was why the company continued to give us plenty of time off between flights. Or in most cases they did. They wouldn't have done that if they felt it wasn't necessary, in order to maintain the crew's good health. That was one of the nice things about being on a flight crew. We usually averaged two weeks of flight duty and two weeks off to rest and recuperate. Maybe that's why two of our children have flown for an airline for over 25 years. Good job!

For the rest of 1946 and all of 1947 I did nothing but fly to all the familiar cities around the world but spent less and less time in any of them. I made only a few more B-314 flights and had stopped flying the Navy flights altogether. The flying boat era had stopped for me in late 1946. I missed the slower and more leisure flights but especially the lazy, laidback layover times we used to have.

The company had definitely switched to landplanes at this point in time. There were now enough daily schedules to most major cities that we would fly 10 or 12 hours, layover for a nights rest. The next day take the inbound flight to the next couple of cities and layover another day. We covered greater distances as land planes flew at 270 MPH. My flights were mostly on the Lockheed L049 with only two or three on the Douglas DC-4 to San Juan, and Belem, where we would met the Rio based crews.

I was sorry I didn't get to go on the inaugural flight around the world but someone more senior to me went instead. The flight was PAA's first commercial round the world flight that took off from La Guardia Airport June 29, 1947. It was made on the L049 Clipper America, NC86520, skippered by Capt. Hugh Gordon and carried 20 passengers. The global flight took 92:42 minutes and took 12 days. They stopped in 10 countries and 17 cities in its 20,000 mile trip. This is when the company began a weekly schedule in both easterly and westerly directions.

About this time, I had heard there was a possibility of a transfer to the Pacific Division. Also I was told the flying was so much smoother with less wintertime bad weather fronts to fly through. Anyway I had had almost enough of the Atlantic Division so Florence and I decided to submit our bid for San Francisco (SFO). It was early spring 1948, before we were told we'd be transferred to SFO.

Boeing 377 *Clipper America* was the first commercial airliner to serve Operation Deep Freeze, shown at McMurdo Sound, Antarctica, October 15, 1957. Pan American World Airways painting by John mcCoy.

Chapter 29

First International Clipper Landed at Bradley International on Instruments

Another first for me was when I was returning from London on a Connie. It was March 1948. We'd left Gander for La Guardia and were just passing over Boston, when ATC told us that La Guardia was closed due to weather minimums and suggested we divert to an alternate airport: Bradley Airport in Hartford. That was news for us as none of the bigger airliners had ever landed there before.

Bradley had just completed an extensive expansion of runways and the installation of an instrument landing system (ILS). We checked in with Hartford approach control and told them we planned to divert from La Guardia to Hartford. They told us that since we would be the first transatlantic "heavy" on their new long runway, we were to pull the power back to slow our approach and go into a holding pattern. We were puzzled about that for a moment. The next transmission Approach Control told us that the local new TV station in Hartford had been told of our arrival and asked if it was at all possible to delay our landing for about 15 minutes, to give the TV station a chance to get their remote pickup unit out to the airport to film our arrival live. We said sure.

We switched to the tower frequency and began to get all kinds of exciting messages, while we were in the holding pattern. Essentially we were told that both radio station WTIC and the new local TV station were set up and we could start our descent. I felt this was big time for us and I guess so did the rest of the crew. I was told later that all the passengers were delighted too, after they had groaned and moaned about having to land at Hartford and would miss the people that had expected to meet them in New York.

We assured them that all passengers would be immediately bussed to La Guardia and that our diversion had been announced over the PA system at La Guardia terminal. That was routine for the company to move the passengers to their destination just as fast as possible and telling them where their baggage could hopefully be located later.

The Bradley weather was light rain but above minimums. The skipper chose to try out the ILS instrument landing system anyway. I had noticed that the pilots had both gotten their landing approach chart out and had been studying it carefully. The ILS approach had worked OK. We touched down easily and slowly taxied toward the ramp. At the last moment we were waved off the ramp and told to stop there. We guessed it was to give the TV cameras a chance to get us at the best angle. Ground control finally told us to cut our engines and the ground crew rolled a moveable ramp in place.

As the passengers disembarked they were asked if they minded being interviewed and most everyone accepted. The TV camera crew and radio reporters with mikes began to overwhelm the passengers. Obviously when Captain Warren stepped out of the plane, he became the center of attention. Later the rest of us had our moment of glory too. I suppose a great deal of what the cameras and reporters picked up was repetitious. But this was big news and they all seemed hungry to get every word. After all we were the first to land there on a flight from Europe. Big deal. Being the newly expanded "Bradley International Airport", most anything anyone said was acceptable and went on the air. This was well before a video tape recording was available so everything was live.

The passengers were soon herded into two waiting Greyhound busses and took off for New York. We crew waited round for a decision on what to do and hoped the New York weather would improve so we could fly the plane home. In the meantime the local Cessna FBO owner taxied one of his newest alongside the Connie and up under our left wing. I think I have a photo of that somewhere. The contrast in size was quite dramatic, of course.

The owner offered any of the crew a chance for a few minutes flight around Hartford. I was the first one to accept. He must have assumed we were all pilots because as soon as we got clearance to take off from the tower, he said "Go ahead and takeoff son" If anyone really knew me then (or now) you would know that I obviously had said sure.

Adrenaline began to pump as I pushed the throttles forward and we began to zigzag down the middle of the runway. I had never made a takeoff before and hadn't realized just how much torque the spinning prop created. The plane kept wanting to run off the runway but I knew enough to keep pushing harder on the opposite rudder to keep us on the center line. At long last I got it steadied. The air speed climbed to 65 and I pulled back on the wheel. We left the runway and started to climb. I was equally scared, excited and thrilled all at the same time. Quickly, I shouted to the guy, where should I steer. I wasn't about to tell him I had never flown a light plane before. All my mini flying had been "straight and level" flying the Clippers at several thousand feet in the air, over the ocean and no one around to fly into. Plus I had a friendly competent commercial pilot with thousands of flight hours sitting beside me. It was different I can tell you!!! After climbing a bit more he told me to level off and make a 180 turn. I know I must have been sweating and began to be quite frightened. I asked the pilot to take over "so I could see some of the city at that low altitude". I thought that was a good excuse for me to get out that scary mess. I hadn't wanted him to tell me to go ahead, turn around

Pan American auto plate

and land. NO WAY. Obviously he took over, checked with the tower and did a normal approach and landed, with a big sigh of relief from me.

Hours later, New York weather cleared and we happily climbed aboard and flew home.

Chapter 30

My Inaugural Flight to Johannesburg - Atlantic Skippers Listed

One of the last flights in the Atlantic Division was kind of a thrilling one for me. I was assigned to one more of the inaugural flights that PAA often made. This one was from New York to Johannesburg, South Africa.

We left La Guardia on a L049 Connie with Capt. Warren on Feb. 25, 1948. We had 20 VIPs on board who were Metropolitan newspaper publishers from all over the U. S. The flight would stop at the Azores and Dakar then nonstop to Jo-Berg. It would cut the flight time by four hours twenty minutes and eliminate the Lisbon stop.

What made this trip so important was that Trippe had been making a big publicity splash about this inaugural flight for political reasons. He wanted to show that PAA was continuing to expand steadily, in the face of growing Atlantic competi-

tion. He had carefully chosen some of the most influential city newspaper publishers he thought could help him and do the most good for the company.

When we arrived in Jo-burg, the South African Government had rolled out the red carpet for our passengers. The flight crew was included in the festivities as well. One of my first impressions of Johannesburg was the masses of blacks everywhere and lots of poverty and poor housing that I observed going from the airport to the hotel. Saw only a hand full of whites, who of course were bossing everyone around. Not a particular good impression from my personal point of view.

After checking into a first class hotel, all of us were treated to a fine, lengthy dinner with lots of toasts and drinks. I believe most of the passengers were quietly poured into their beds that night, if I'm not mistaken.

The next morning we were called early for a special treat, for the publishers and us crew members. The treat was again sponsored by the South African Government. We filled one of their local twin engined planes and took off for a two day excursion to Cape Town. For the life of me I remember very little about that visit. All I do recall was that it seemed we were eating and drinking all the time. Those publishers had hollow legs when it came to the booze. Or that was my perception at least. The crew, with mighty restraint, seemed sober to me. I personally have never been much of a drinker, one drink often would give me a powerful headache. And I didn't enjoy it that much. So I've never had any trouble hanging in there with the usual ginger ale or coke. All I can say was, the publishers appeared to be having a fine time and supposedly wrote a lot of nice things about South Africa. I enjoyed our private tour of Cape Town a lot.

The company had spent lots of money on these publishers and particularly to return to New York ON TIME. Trippe set up a complex plan to insure that this would happen. On our return trip from Johannesburg we'd have to arrive in New York March 8, 1948, in order to make the 6 o'clock national news LIVE for the TV networks. This required some extensive and expensive planning on the part of flight scheduling.

Pan Am did an unprecedented thing. A spare Connie was placed at Santa Maria empty, as a backup in case our plane had any problems on the inbound legs to New York. The return flight to New York went smoothly until after we had left Santa Maria. The usual strong headwinds were stronger than forecast so we began to run a few minutes behind schedule. The skipper checked with the Flight Engineer and it was decided to increase the engine RPMs from long range cruise to high speed cruise. We made up 25 minutes before we landed in Bermuda.

After a fast "pit stop" in Bermuda we took off again. Skipper Warren decided to use high speed cruise all the way into to New York, 3 hours time. One hour out, we were still ten minutes behind when the skipper called for takeoff power which is never used except for just a short while, to get the plane off the runway. The power was always cut back right after lift off, otherwise the engines would overheat badly. The Flight Engineer was very worried about the overheating engines and made it very clear to the skipper, it was dangerous to continue doing what we were doing. The engine temperatures hovered just below "red line" but held there.

The whole crew was sweating, as we all knew how much hung on our precise arrival. The big question was; should we pull back the power to prevent damaging the engines but miss our most important deadline. Or should we keep at takeoff power, probably make the schedule but invite engine fires and a major disaster. What a quandary to be in. The Skipper gambled and stayed with takeoff power and won. God, the good angels or the four sturdy 2250 HP Wright Cyclone engines got us into New York and ON TIME! I know the company, Trippe and our publisher passengers were delighted with the fine TV coverage. Obviously I suspect each of us crew were privately greatly relieved that our arrival hadn't turned into a disaster. I never heard about any repercussions from the overheated engines.

Somewhere I have a wallet, that I received as a gift from the publishers, gold embossed with my name and the date of the inaugural flight to Jo-burg, Mar. 8, 1948. Later, I got a publicity photo and news release from the company that gave my company history. It said I was a highly experienced Flight Radio Officer with over 9,000 flight hours and had crossed the Atlantic 140 times. How about that?.

Before I start on the transfer to San Francisco, I'd like to list some of the Atlantic Division Captains I flew with, using my log book. One of the interesting things Flight Scheduling did was to make up the flight crews on a random basis. The company felt that it was best done that way and I don't remember exactly why. There were several hundred Captains so we seldom flew with the same skipper more than once or twice over the six plus years I was in New York.

Ed Sommers was the one Skipper I got to fly with five times. Just a fluke I guess. Dick Vinal was another pilot I luckily few with several times.

All Pan Am Captains with one or two exceptions, were really terrific pilots and real gentlemen. They were proud and ego-tistical men but deserved to be respected as they had spent long years of extensive training and had become the best and safest pilots in the world.

When a Captain finally checked out as "Master of Ocean Flying" they were tops in aviation piloting internationally. They had many thousands of flight hours, licenses in aircraft and engines, radiotelegraph code (CW) and had completed many courses in meteorology, world wide navigation, international diplomacy and other varied subjects. They all were "Top Aces" in my opinion.

Some credit for PAAs great pilots should go to Priester for his careful pilot hiring practices, along with the high standards he had set for his original flight crews. His crew performance manual was famous in the company. Many jokes were made about it but the fact remained, it was a darn good set of rules. Priester ran a tight ship from the beginning, which kept future flight crew performance up to snuff.

Here's my list of a great and proud bunch of guys and the ones I flew with for over six years. The big multiple crews of the Atlantic Division was where I learned about true team work, flying on the large Boeing B314 flying boat. Before and after this period we had the three and four man cockpit crews. I think the intense sense of responsibility we each had about the safety of the flight never really changed regardless of crew size. Skippers I had flown with in New York included:

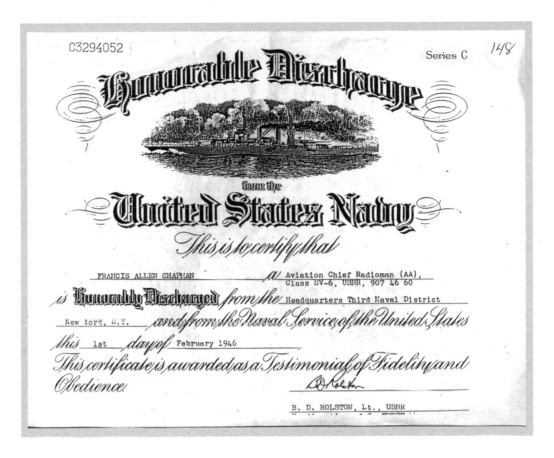

The end of World War II released Pan Am personnel from their obligations to the U. S. Navy. Chapman frequently ferried Navy aircraft across the Atlantic during the war when not on Pan Am flights. Frank Chapman

The jet age sparked a boom in air travel bringing the whole world within hours of each other. Evening flights to Europe have only a few hours of darkness before the five or six hour time difference heralds the dawn of a new day. Photo shows a Pan Am 707 enroute to Schipol and Hamburg. Hal Carstens

Bassett	Hart	Cone
Lewis	McCullough	DeLima
Lodensen	McLaughlin	Dugan
LaPorte	Mitchell	Durst
Mattis	Nolan	Fleming
Masland	O'Connor	Fordyce
Pippinger	Goodwin	Schoder
Gray	Smith	Gulbransen
Somers	Szmagaj	Vaugh
Vinal	Weber	Winston

Chapter 31

San Francisco Calling- Developing the Pacific

Along about March, 1948, the company decided it was okay for our transfer to San Francisco. We had built a Cape Cod dream house on Lawrence Hill Rd. in Cold Spring Harbor, L.I. We four; Florence, Allan, Kenneth and I were so sorry to be moving away from a lovely new house. But that's the way life often is. So we had the movers come in and away we went to another new experience of living in California and flying all over the Pacific.

Jeanne Elizabeth Arrived - June 24, 1948

Our family of 4 was about to be increased to 5, with the birth of our daughter Jeanne Elizabeth. So we were anxious to get settled fast. We found a small new two bedroom home at 372 Parma Ave. Los Altos, Ca. 35 miles south of San Francisco.

Florence delivered a charming, warm and cuddly gem of a daughter at the Palo Alto Hospital with no complications, date, June 24, 1948. She was something very special from the very beginning and immediately captivated absolutely everyone including her two big brothers. She was loved and adored by all, especially me. Her name is Jeanne Elizabeth. And what made it so nice was I was there to greet and hold her minutes after she arrived. Mm, lovely!

A brief history of the Pacific Division, before I get started with my flights there. Lindberg officially surveyed an Alaskan route a few months after his solo flight of the Atlantic in 1927. Soon after he completed his survey flight, all the way to Moscow, he reported to Trippe that it was essential to have good navigation and radio facilities around the polar region in order to safely fly that route. As usual Trippe promptly took Lindberg seriously and established radio facilities and meteorological stations throughout Alaska that reported to him regularly in New York. At the same time, he had negotiation with the Soviet Government to fly over Siberia and got approval. In exchange, Trippe agreed to build permanent hangars along the route and to train Russian pilots. He finally merged two small Alaskan Airlines into one called Pacific Alaska Airways. This was the nucleus of the Pacific Division.

Also at about this same time Trippe was trying to get approval to land in Australia, a British Commonwealth, and got nowhere. However, he again proved to be politically savvy and was able to convince New Zealand, a British Commonwealth as well, to let Pan Am land there. And as Trippe expected, it wasn't very long after flights began going into New Zealand that the Australian government had a change of heart. They quickly offered to let Pan Am land at Sydney as well. The Australian business world didn't want to be second to anyone, especially New Zealand, when it came to getting direct routes to the United States.

Trippe played the same game when Hong Kong refused PAA landing rights, with behind the scenes urging from the British. So he got Macao, a Portuguese island possession nearby, to grant him landing rights. This put him within easy reach of China and connections with his subsidy airline Chinese National Airlines Corp (CNAC) that had been operating successfully. Soon after flights began going into Macao, Hong Kong did an about face, advising Trippe that landing in their city was now permitted. Despite the continual road blocks that the British had placed in Trippe's way, his expansion moved onward.

However, all was not rosy for our intrepid leader elsewhere. Troubles began to pile up. Pacific Alaska Airways had operated all winter long in temperatures averaging minus 50 degree with major maintenance problems. The Bolshevik government refused to pay the U. S. Government monies owed and refused PAA permission to cross Siberia. So Trippe decided to close the division until things improved.

There also were big problems in the Atlantic as well. The British continued to have their own problems in getting their aircraft equipment ready to cross the Atlantic. As I may have mentioned earlier, Pan Am and British Airways had been struggling to live up to their five year old agreement to begin Atlantic crossings simultaneously. It appeared the British would still be unable to cross the Atlantic for about two more years, even though Pan Am was ready to start then.

Pan Am had already completed several successful survey flights across the Atlantic in the Sikorsky S-42. So Trippe's dilemma was in determining what direction he should extend his world expansion efforts. He chose to try crossing the 9,000 mile wide Pacific and connect with his own CNAC operation. His sights were still set on a Global airline.

In mid 1934, he had three S-42's and three new Martin M-130's readied to fly the Pacific. Again Trippe did more of his secret and fancy negotiations with old friends in the government, and got Navy approval for the company to land at Midway, Wake and Guam islands on the way to Manila and Hong Kong. After much careful planning, he had assembled men and a massive amount of equipment, and sent them to Midway and Wake atolls to establish seaplane bases.

Chapter 32

China Clipper's Inaugural Flight to Orient Via Hawaii, Midway, Wake, Guam and Manila

The stage was now set for still another first. This inaugural flight would establish the first airmail route from the United States to China and ports in the Far East. Time was Nov. 22, 1935.

Captain Ed Musick was the skipper on the new Martin M-130 which left Alameda for Hawaii, on the first leg of the inaugural flight. Trippe had made a massive effort to publicize this trip. He had many newspapers alerted and all major radio networks, standing by live to cover the departure, along with seven radio networks in Europe, South America and the Orient.

Thus began an aviation history event which linked six islands and hopped over the Pacific to the Orient. This flight opened up a new era in world aviation. The Martin M-130 was aptly called the China Clipper. It took off with 110,865 letters and seven winged pioneers as flight crew.

Veteran Flight Radio Officer Bill Jarboe was on board. (He later became Communications Superintendent of the Atlantic Division) Other bigwig flight crew aboard were First Officer Captain Sullivan, Fred Noonan, PAA's first master mariner and Navigator and two top Flight Engineers C. D. Wright and Victor Wright along with George King, 2nd pilot officer. Of course Skipper Musick headed the whole bunch. A power house flight crew.

The skipper took off from Alameda so full of gas that he wasn't able to climb over the partly finished Oakland-San Francisco Bay bridge so flew UNDER it as if it had been planned that way. He finally began a slow banking turn to the southwest and gained altitude, just clearing the towers of the unfinished Golden Gate Bridge. He continued climbing to his cruising altitude.

The flight to Honolulu covered 2,410 miles and took them 21:04 hours. They had had a clear night flight, with plenty of celestial sights taken by Fred Noonan and good radio commu-

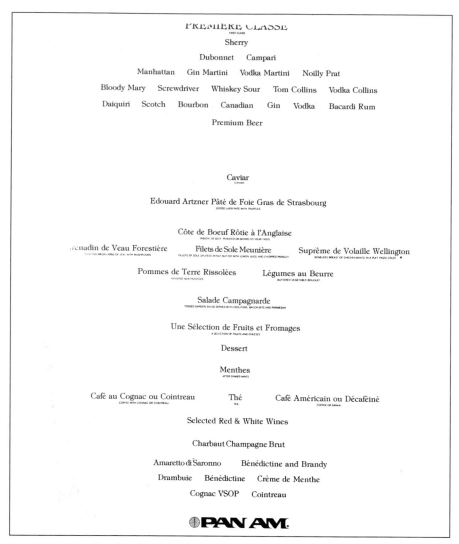

PREMIERE CLASSE
FIRST CLASS

Sherry

Dubonnet   Campari

Manhattan   Gin Martini   Vodka Martini   Noilly Prat

Bloody Mary   Screwdriver   Whiskey Sour   Tom Collins   Vodka Collins

Daiquiri   Scotch   Bourbon   Canadian   Gin   Vodka   Bacardi Rum

Premium Beer

Caviar
CAVIAR

Edouard Artzner Pâté de Foie Gras de Strasbourg
GOOSE LIVER PATE WITH TRUFFLES

Côte de Boeuf Rôtie à l'Anglaise
FILLET OF BEEF ROASTED ON BOARD TO YOUR TASTE

Grenadin de Veau Forestière   Filets de Sole Meunière   Suprême de Volaille Wellington
SELECTED MEDALLIONS OF VEAL WITH MUSHROOMS   FILLETS OF SOLE SAUTEED IN NUT BUTTER WITH LEMON JUICE AND CHOPPED PARSLEY   BONELESS BREAST OF CHICKEN BAKED IN A PUFF PASTE CRUST

Pommes de Terre Rissolées   Légumes au Beurre
ROASTED NEW POTATOES   BUTTERED VEGETABLE BOUQUET

Salade Campagnarde
TOSSED GARDEN SALAD SERVED WITH CROUTONS, BACON BITS AND PARMESAN

Une Sélection de Fruits et Fromages
A SELECTION OF FRUITS AND CHEESES

Dessert

Menthes
AFTER DINNER MINTS

Café au Cognac ou Cointreau   Thé   Café Américain ou Décaféiné
COFFEE WITH COGNAC OR COINTREAU   TEA   COFFEE OR SANKA

Selected Red & White Wines

Charbaut Champagne Brut

Amaretto di Saronno   Bénédictine and Brandy
Drambuie   Bénédictine   Crème de Menthe
Cognac VSOP   Cointreau

⊛ PAN AM.

Pan Am's blue box lunches of cold, greasy chicken and rice had long given way to superb cuisine the equivalent of anything found in fine restaurants on the ground. This menu was on a Boeing 707 flight. Collection of Hal Carstens

nications with Alameda, Los Angles, Honolulu and Midway, according to FRO Wilson (Bill) Jarboe. The next morning they took off again with loads of Thanksgiving food for both Midway and Wake personnel. They flew along under some low hanging rain squalls at 2,000 feet and landed safely on the lagoon next to the tiny barren island which was Midway. The flight took 7:59 minutes.

Once more the China Clipper lifted off just after sunrise and headed west for Wake crossing the International date line and lost a day. They covered the 1252 miles in 8:05 hours averaging 149 MPH. The landing area was a shallow lagoon filled with lots of corral heads which the ground personnel had been steadily working to reduce.

The next two legs, Wake to Guam and Guam to Manila went without any major incidences. But the crew was not expecting the huge crowds who were there to meet the Clipper when it touched down on Manila Harbor at 3:32 pm, Nov. 29, 1935. The plane had covered 8,210 miles Alameda-Manila, Philippines in 59:48 hours flying time and seven days.

When the crew stepped ashore, they were met with loud cheers. When Capt Musick was asked how was the flight, his reply was "without incident". How's that for a brief and cryptic response?

At that point in time, that was as far west as they could fly, as approval to land in mainland China had not been received. Later flights were able to get into the islands of Macao and Hong Kong.

So after a three day layover in Manila, the inaugural flight returned to California. It took them four hours longer in total flight time, on the Manila-Guam leg, as they had encountered 70 MPH head winds.

Chapter 33

North to Fairbanks

Now I have to admit, I'm badly organized. I have done an extensive search of my cluttered research materials here, and I'm unable to find my tiny flight log book that covers the Pacific Division flights. So I won't have my aircraft numbers, FROs or skippers names or flying times. In the past the log has been a great help in triggering my memory on my trips. I'll do my best without the logbook.

The San Francisco International Airport was located in the Bay, adjacent to San Mateo and was called Mills Field. The first time I drove there from Los Altos it took me 40 minutes. In 1948, route 101 was very busy. I was able to get to the airport quickly. The 101 by-pass hadn't built then.

It was two weeks after we had arrived in the San Francisco area that they put me on the flight schedule. We had had a chance to close on the house and had settled in. As usual, Flo went to work to make the new house a home. She had a special knack and skill in that area. Colorful curtains, matching living room slip covers. All those nice things for comfortable and cheery living.

My first trip was a special one to Fairbanks, Alaska with intermediate stops at Ketchikan and Juneau. It was on a Boeing B377 Stratocruiser that cruised at 275 MPH. Total flight time for the 2200 miles, SFO-FAI, was about 9 hours. I only made this one flight, I think it had VIP's aboard but I don't recall.

This first flight to Fairbanks was in June 1948 and I was totally unprepared for the heat and huge mosquitoes that attacked everyone. I had imagined, as most people who have never been to that state before, that it was cold all year long. Wrong. Fairbanks can be minus 50 degrees in the dead of winter, but in the summer it is in the 90's with those aggressive biters with wings.

Chapter 34

Across the Vast Blue Pacific To Hong Kong, Bangkok, Sydney and Tokyo

I was in the Pacific Division a little over a year, spring 1948 to summer 1949. During that time I was assigned a dozen or so long flights to different cities, before I left the company.

My memories of some places I went to are not so vivid simply because I only went to them once. And that meant I had just an overnight, where I slept most of the time I was there. Honolulu was the garden of Eden spot I visited about fifteen times. The Pacific Division flights would take me to destinations like Hong kong, Bangkok, Tokyo, and Sydney, Australia. I never landed at Auckland, New Zealand but I was told the North Island was beautiful.

Some of those extended flights were on the L049 Connie, with a 3,000 mile range, and speed of 260 MPH; plus a few on the B-377 Stratocruiser, with a range of 3,200 miles and speed of 275 MPH. So we got everywhere much faster but the distances were greater over the Pacific compared to the Atlantic. For example, the distance to Hong kong from SFO was about 9,000 miles versus the Atlantic, N. Y. to London about 3,000 miles.

The various islands that we landed at in crossing the wide Pacific were quite different. The Hawaiian Islands had been well established for over three hundred years, populated with a great number of beautiful people from all over the Pacific and the Orient. Honolulu had fine roads, airports, industry, a balanced economy in a gorgeous setting of wild flowers, fruit and plenty of food grown locally, with friendly open people. The climate was mild and tropical, no extremes, 60 to 90 degrees year round.

Trippe had worked his magic planning and negotiating with the Navy, all of which he had put into action in 1934/35. Those two tiny islands of Midway and Wake became key air bases for Pan Am to use. Thus PAA could hop, skip and jump over the vast Pacific to the Orient. All of this magnificent advanced planning had been in preparation for the China Clipper's historical inaugural flight to the Far East in late 1935.

So when I came along 13 years later, all those little barren islands in the Pacific had a look of permanence. Midway, Wake and Guam, had good overnight accommodations, plenty of food, water, adequate runways, fuel aplenty, communications and Adcock DF bearing facilities that covered the Pacific very well. Some of the radio pioneering that I had helped with over the past nine years in the Latin American and Atlantic Divisions, had all been done before I arrived. Even though the distances were much greater, it looked as if our flights would work rather smoothly. And they did. I continued to be lucky with no minor or major disasters during my last year with the company.

It seemed as if a little bit of the excitement and the early thrills had drifted into being somewhat routine flying. I guess I was preparing myself for change, away from all the glamour and delight of international air travel.

All Pacific flights except the Alaskan ones started out via Hawaii. I got to be very fond of Honolulu, Oahu and the Moana Hotel at Waikiki. The beach was lovely, swimming in that beautiful warm water was glorious, the temperatures superb and girl watching extraordinary. Having Stewardesses on board and gaggles of them from other flights laying over at the Moana helped kept life interesting for all of us men. Is that a chauvinist remark? Guess I'm in trouble if I have to ask.

One of my first trips over the Pacific was aboard a L049 Connie to Hong Kong via Honolulu, Midway, Wake, Guam and Manila. The distance from SFO to HNL was 2,410 miles and usually took 9 to 10 hours flight time.

After our overnight at the Moana on Waikiki Beach, we took off to the Northwest for Midway, 1,350 miles away, which was the smallest island in the chain. It took us 5 or 6 hours to do that leg. The tiny island was 2 miles long and a mile wide. Their were a few Navy Quonset huts and lots of goony birds. Those birds didn't seem able to fly but just waddled around. They loved to sit on the cement runways for some unknown reason. The airport maintenance guys would have to speed up and down the runway in their jeep, to clear it, before we could land or take off. Unbelievably dumb birds. They were called frigate birds.

Then we headed for Wake, 1,260 miles to the west. That flight was slightly shorter and took about 5 hours. We overnighted there in very passable housing. Wake was a slightly larger V shaped island 5 miles long and surrounded by a corral reef that formed a lagoon, where the B-314 and S-42 sea planes used to land. The company had been able to squeeze out a nicely paved runway on the beach along one side of the V. PAA had built wooden buildings to house overnight passengers and the permanent PAA personnel. Beside the basic necessities for survival, Wake had nothing else but sand and the vast ocean all around. The personnel complained about their loneliness which was a very legitimate gripe.

The hop on the third day took us to Guam, 1,560 miles further to the west. This was a good sized island 20 miles long and 5 miles wide, with about 15,000 people. It was mountainous but there was a well established Naval base. The next stop was at Manila 1,620 miles away and then on to Hong Kong, 700 miles further Northwest.

Hong Kong and Bangkok were to me, the most oriental and fascinating cities I had been to so far. Hong Kong still had the strong British influence, although it had retained its own ancient Chinese culture as well. An interesting mix. I'm not sure the British made a great change in its culture except in the way of doing business and introducing their monetary system. The business world had been changed to an open economy.

It was a shoppers paradise since there were no taxes or duty charges for the tourists. I bought my first Rolex Oyster month/day chronometer watch there for $50. I proudly wore it until someone stole it from me at a hotel in Milan, when I was on a business trip many years later.

I believe the British encouraged the use of opium in Hong Kong from the beginning and it had grown into a monumental multibillion pound trade, even in the '40s. It's believed also that is why there are hundreds of banks and worldwide businesses established there.

I was told that the boat people live their entire lives on the junks permanently anchored in a crowded mass in the harbor. That hasn't changed in centuries.

The airport was situated in the only flat space that extended into the harbor. It's located where there is a small mountain at one end of the runway. On our arrival the Skipper had to just clear the peak and then quite literally make a fairly steep dive to touch down at the beginning of the runway and then stand on the brakes hard so as not to run off the other end. That was kind of a scary thrill.

I don't recall about the hotel or anything special as to where we ate. I do remember how crowded everything seemed and people were in a huge hurry. I didn't do any touring that I recall. Bangkok was another fascinating city to see. Oh my, but it was hot there. A few things that stood out about that city during my brief visit were its breathtaking Buddhist temples. The few people I met and saw seemed to have a quiet and peaceful aura about them. The features of the tiny women were lovely and their movements graceful.

Another very long trip I flew was the one to Sydney via Honolulu, and the Fiji Islands. After an overnight at the Moana, we took off south for the long direct flight to Viti Levu landing at Suva. It was 3,176 miles over the peaceful Pacific and took about 12 hours to get there. This probably was the longest distance over water that I had ever flown. By this time the newer version of the Connie had been delivered to the company. It was designated the L749 which had bigger engines giving it a longer range and better speed, about 282 MPH. The cockpit crew was down to four.

We used to land at Suva but apparently the present day jets now land at Nadi. This was a truly lovely place with its soft and pleasant temperatures and laid back people. The main island of the Fiji chain is Viti Levu and is a British possession. Its over 75 miles long and has a good sized mountain range. We flight crew played a lot of tennis and ping-pong to get our exercise before we turned in for the night. It seemed to me we had two day layovers a couple of times, due to the way the weekly schedules were set up. I definitely recall having my old friend Captain Ed Somers from Seattle as Skipper on one of those flights. He was another skipper that I had become fairly close too. I admired him a lot. He was a great pilot who was quiet spoken and radiated a great deal of confidence. We played lots of tennis together. That's a place I definitely want to return to some day soon.

The final leg to Sydney was 1,969 miles and took 7 hours. Sydney is a spirited, clean, modern cosmopolitan city with what seemed to be thousands of sailboats everywhere. The city was built around the fine harbor with its spectacular bridge spanning the harbor. The Australian people all seemed to me to be cherry, healthy and happy. That's a bold statement but was my perception anyway. The total flight time from San Francisco to Sydney, was a bit over 40 hours with overnights in Honolulu and Suva.

One of the last flights I made was my one and only trip to Tokyo via Honolulu and, Midway. That was aboard the B-377 Stratocruiser, which was a bit more luxurious than the Connie and about 5 MPH faster. The Loran equipment was a pleasure to operate. The Northern Pacific was well covered by Loran signals, so all flights into Tokyo were able to get fine position fixes. The distance was about the same as from SFO to HNL and took the same flight time 9:30 minutes

Tokyo is another spectacular Oriental city of polite, charming people but with an oh so very crowded downtown business district. About the only thing I remember about my overnight there was being shown the Emperor's Palace, on the way to the hotel. The Japanese appeared to be most industrious and busy, with thousands of bicycles coming at you, in all directions. My one impression of Tokyo was they had run out of space to build on. They needed a few more millions of acres to be able to spread out some. The B-377 flight time from San Francisco to Tokyo took about 25 hours.

Chapter 35

A Sad Parting but Good Job Hunting

Pan Am ticket for Flight No. 205 on June 11, 1970 from New York's John F. Kennedy Airport to Nassau, Puerto Rico, with return on Flight 206 on June 17, 1970. Aircraft was a Boeing 707. The flying boats and propeller aircraft had long disappeared. Collection of Hal Carstens

Pan American Airways had been very good to me. I began as a shy young man from New Hampshire with few real life experiences and little confidence. Ten years later, I had become a more sophisticated, experienced and mature man. I had flown around the world to old cities and new, helped in a small way, blaze new aviation trails. I'd lived in Rio and other fascinating cities in the U. S., had learned team work, gained more knowledge of aviation communications, piloting, navigation and meteorology.

I was certainly going to miss all the wonderful tiring flights. Especially my six weeks vacation with the good salary. Most of all, I'd miss the usual two weeks off each month for R and R. It was such a delight to spend that length of time with Florence and the children. I wasn't going to miss the emotional tug of leaving dearest Flo and each youngster, as we said good-bye before each trip. I was content to hang up my uniform and shuck my cap and shiny black shoes for good.

All of the flight crews based in SFO had been hearing the scuttlebutt. Some of the Navigators had already been released and we FROs knew that our time was short. Finally May 1st, 1949, the company announced that the FROs were being asked to leave. Because I had a high seniority number, I was offered two choices to stay with Pan Am. One was to work in the company SFO air to ground radio station handling traffic with inflight aircraft and company stations throughout the Pacific. The second choice I had was to transfer to Rio and fly as a Supernumerary flight crew member, LOGGING all cockpit to ground radiotelephone conversations. The ground station position didn't appeal to me very much. Nor being transferred to Rio with our three young children didn't appeal, in fact it sounded BORING!

After a brief family discussion, I told the company I would accept my severance for ten years of service. It was kind of sad for me to leave my favorite airline. I had grown up in the com-

pany and had had such great times flying with terrific men. My experiences had been special, but I still had unforgettable memories. Had been hard work, at times very exhausting, even scary. But I felt I was ready for a change.

In the spring of 1949,. I proceeded to look for a job. The first possibility was with the new TV station about to go on the air in San Francisco, KRON-TV. I interviewed for the Radio Station Engineer. My FCC Radiotelephone license qualified me.

About that same time my friend FRO Freddy Mathews called me late one night. He said he had just been interviewed by a guy named George Arnold from Fairchild Camera and Instrument Corp. Freddy said they were looking for Electronic Field Service Engineers for Northern California. He suggested that I call him. Even though it was something like 8 PM, my assertive nature took over and I phoned the St. Francis Hotel in San Francisco. The tired sounding voice on the other end said it was really too late for an interview. He said he was headed back to his home office in New York in the morning. I must have used some of my budding and persuasive salesmanship such as I could be there within 30 minutes and felt I was extremely well qualified for the job. He sleepily agreed to see me so I raced into the city.

I rapped on his hotel room door about 45 minutes later. After he let me in he collapsed onto the bed and proceeded to interview me lying down. I realize now but didn't know then, that he had probably drank his dinner. Anyway he had electronic schematics strewn all over the floor. He said I was the 26th man he'd interviewed that day and asked me several questions like would I mind driving 35,000 miles a year servicing electro-mechanical engraving machines in newspapers. I'm sure I said I would be delighted to do that kind of driving. After a few more questions, he pointed at the schematics on the floor and said did I know what that represented. I said

As flag carrier of the United States, Pan American World Airways served the world but was denied the ability to service domestic flights. The pioneers who worked for Pan Am daily risked their lives in primitive flying machines. In time, their efforts made Pan Am flying boats opened the oceans to safe, speedy air travel. Pan American World Airways.

sure, it looked like a power supply and a 100 watt audio amplifier. That seemed to satisfy him. It was a very brief interview. He said he would get in touch with me if he was interested in hiring me and I left.

The good news was, I received a telegram a week later that said I was hired as a Field Service Engineer for Northern California. I would be paid $150. a week plus expenses. I'd get a new company car each year and could use it for personal use if I put in my own gas. I was told to report to Jamaica, Long Island, immediately for five weeks of factory training on their new Fairchild Scanagraver, an electronic photoengraving machine being leased to newspapers nationally. This meant I would have to take a crash course in photography and newspaper printing methods. I was very happy to accept the job as it sounded challenging. During my first week of my Fairchild training in Jamaica, Flo phoned me to say I had been called by KRON-TV to come in for a second interview and would probably be offered a job. I obviously had to tell them I already had a job.

I worked for Fairchild for 20 years moving from Field Service Engineer to District Service Manager, Assistant National Service Manager and finally to the National Service Managers spot. I took over the job George Arnold had. He was the man who had hired me 20 years earlier.

To digress one last time to describe the demise of Pan Am, on Dec. 4, 1991. Pan American World Airways had its LAST flight, when the newest of Boeing's 727, Clipper Goodwill, left Bridgetowne, Barbados and headed for the city where Pan Am had started 64 years earlier, Miami. This closed a chapter in world aviation that had its meager beginning when PAAs inaugural flight took off from Key West for Havana in 1927. PAA died after a spectacular rise and explosive expansion, which regularly made history in the world of international aviation. The consensus as to why PAA collapsed seemed to be "inept management, indifferent government and extremely heavy airline competition both from domestic as well as the world"

I quote some paragraphs from the article "The Last Clipper" that Pan Am Captain Mark Pyle, the skipper of the Clipper Goodwill wrote in the Airline Pilot magazine of June 1992 about the last landing in Miami.

"As we taxied past the first formations, men and women came to a brisk attention and saluted `the last of the Clippers`.

Tears welled up in my eyes then for the first time. Many rows of people and machines-all smartly formed-all saluted. I returned the salute just as crisply, fully knowing that their salutes were to this `machine` and to all the machines` that bore the title `Clipper` for 64 years. Their salute was to the history that this ship represented and to all that had gone before."

"We passed the line of fire equipment, and the water cannon was fired over the aircraft. My emotions reeled under the weight of this tribute to Pan Am's last flight. I engaged the windshield wiper to clear the water that was on the windscreen, but that did little good for the water in my eyes. My first officer fought back his tears. He had worn Pan Am blue for 23 years."

"One final formation-all Pan American ground personnel-tendered their last salute. We approached the gate and set the brakes for the last time. We shut down systems for the last time and secured the faithful engines. Sadly gathering our belongings, we shook hands. Our final flight was over. No eyes in the cockpit were dry. Many of the departing passengers shared our moment of grief. The tears will continue."

Chapter 36

A Bit More Personal - Family and Church

Some of you may have wondered what ever became of my romantic story I promised you, concerning my loving, beautiful, charming and delightful wife Florence Ann Rodgers Chapman. After much thought, I've decided that I must apologize to the reader. I don't feel right about relating a lot of my innermost feeling and sensations that race through my mind when I think of Florence. Maybe I'm saying these things are too private and intimate to put down. So let me see if I can tiptoe around the edges a bit but not delve too deeply where my heart is concerned. Okay?

When I first met Flo at Dinner Key in late 1939, I quickly realized, that she was something special and rare. She was the young lady I wanted to marry, love and live with. The chemistry was wonderful between us.

We romanced in lovely Miami and were married in Coconut Grove on May 15, 1940. Thanks to the foreign assignment policy of PAA, within a very short time we were told we were to be transferred to spectacular Rio. We enjoyed what I always called our year long honeymoon. Our year's stay

in Rio passed delightfully fast. Flo was expecting and because her German doctor knew I was to be transferred to New York soon suggested she return to the U. S. Son Allan arrived Aug. 4, 1941 but unfortunately I wasn't there.

One thing you could say about our growing family, we moved a lot. Look at where our children were born. Allan in Miami Beach, Kenny in Glen Head, L. I. and Jeannie in Los Altos, Ca. That's what happens when one worked for an international airline.

When Flo and I were first married, we fell into what was a typical old fashioned marriage. This was where I was supposed to earn the money and she kept the house beautiful and cared for the children. I unknowingly (being a MCP) thought this was the way it was supposed to be. Now I know how wrong I was, but that's what it was like back then. Whenever I was home, and we had a new infant, I'd handle the 2 AM baby feeding. I thought that was very special and intimate for me. And on the other end of the situation, I became proficient with diapers, I let only one get flushed down the drain.

We moved to Glen Cove in 1941, when Allan was 6 months old. We rented an apartment unfurnished so we had to rush out and get a crib for Allan and a bed for ourselves. We used a lot of orange crates and card tables covered with fine linen table clothes we had received for wedding presents.

We had received a great number of presents, like silverware, dishes, kitchenware but no furniture. So for that first year, we had very few places to sit on. It was either the bed or the floor for a while.

Allan being the first baby had 100's of photos taken of him almost every week and in every possible costume from nude to fully dressed with a bonnet! Ken and Jeannie didn't get that kind of photographic coverage. Wonder why?

Flo and I poured over Dr. Spock's baby book on how to bring up baby. I remember saying to myself, what does he know about Allan, every baby is absolutely unique, so wouldn't you need to treat each one differently? At the same time each child wants to be treated fairly and in the same way. "You gave him a lolly pop, I want one too". This sounds kinda dumb to me, treat children as individuals, differently: yet be fair with each and treat them the same. A conflicting and confusing conundrum. I think Florence and I did okay as parents but ultimately our children have to be the final judge. I hope they knew as they were growing up, that they were loved unconditionally by us and we still do.

When Allan was about 6 years old we lived in Floral Park. He had a small accident in our living room. Somehow he fell against a radio receiver that had a glass covering the moving dial indicator. The broken glass cut a modest gash on the side of his nose. I was working in the Communications office at La Guardia, when I got a call from Flo that Allan had cut himself badly and to hurry home. I raced home at 70 MPH via the Cross Island Parkway. Never got a speeding ticket. When I arrived no one was there and the neighbors didn't know anything. I should have realized that Flo in her usual efficient way had taken the appropriate action and gotten Allan to the hospital. Finally they can home and all was well with him. He had a big bandage covering the 4 or 5 stitches. Flo had said that he had been very brave throughout all of it.

We moved from an apartment to our first house, in Glen Head. Kenny was physically very active. He pulled a trick that I didn't like very much when he was about 3. I think he must have just seen me fill the Plymouth with gas. Anyway, he and Allan unscrewed the gas cap and put a handful of sand in the tank then added some water from the garden hose. When I came out to drive the car downtown, I couldn't get it started. The bottom line was I had to get it towed to the gas station and have the tank flushed out. They got no spanking but I told them they'd pulled a big no-no. I wonder if either of them remember.

Jeannie was born in Los Altos so she's one of the original California girls. Our family dog Thursday, adopted her as soon as she started to walk. She would trail along after Jeannie wherever she went. If we could find Thursday, there Jeannie would be.

If someone were to ask me what one personally significant thing had I accomplished during the first ten years of our marriage, I'd say I helped raise the family. But equally important our family had helped build a church.

Los Altos, in 1948, was growing rapidly, and there appeared to be a need for a new church. Flo and I were one of ten families that put in some seed money and harvested hundreds of pounds of apricots that spring to go toward the purchase of 6.6 acres of cow pasture at Parma Ave and Elmonte in Los Altos.

The Methodist Church of Los Altos was begun by ten families. The families had a number of conversations with the Methodist Conference and the Bishop to determine if a real need for a church was appropriate. After a long series of discussions with the bank and the Bishop, we received approval to go ahead with the project.

At long last we were able to buy the land and a young minister Rev. Chuck Cox was called to lead this budding church. We conducted church services out under the tall pin oak trees all that winter. I'll tell you that was such a marvelous spiritual experience for us all. That next spring we broke ground and I personally helped erect our first church building. I became it's first Sunday School Superintendent and Florence taught Sunday school. Obviously, all three of the children attended Sunday school. Soon after that we began building the parsonage.

Some time later the present main sanctuary was built but we weren't there as we had already been transferred to Pasadena, Ca. I believe that first building we built is now the social hall.

Daughter Jeannie currently lives in Oakland and flies for UAL as a flight attendant and earlier had flown for PAA for years. She and I visited the Los Altos church complex in 1991. I had a warm feeling of pride and other emotions that swirled around me, as I walked around the church property with her. I realized that each of our family had put a bit of themselves into that place. It appears to be a great church with its lovely setting in a lowly ex-cow pasture.

When we first moved to Los Altos, I built a 6 foot high redwood fence around our property line. This was to keep the children and dog in our yard. Because of the delightful warm weather we had nearly all year long, we agreed a family swimming pool was needed. We found we had enough room in our back yard, so the 10 by 20 feet pool was personally hand dug 3 to 6 feet deep, by the four of us. Jeannie was still too small to handle a wheel barrow. We did have a little help from a few of our more energetic neighbors. The pool filter I built myself from a 55 gallon oil drum that I had steam cleaned. With some design ideas from the Paddock Pool people, I was able to make a small but effective pool filter.

That leads me into the story about Jeannie when she was two or so. A neighbor who taught swimming, claimed she could teach her to swim at that age. She proceeded to prove it. Within weeks she had Jeannie swimming under water before she was able to swim on top. Jeannie was just like a little pollywog. We felt so much more safe, when we knew she was able to swim. The pool was only a few feet from our back door. So when the warmer weather arrived, most mornings would find all five of us skinny dipping in the pool instead of taking a shower.

A SIMPLE TRIBUTE TO FLORENCE ANN

One more tribute to you, Florence, before I close this memoir. I feel I've lived a happy, busy and productive life. I've been lucky too. But without your loving support, encouragement and understanding, I couldn't have done what I did. You were a loving wife and great Mother to our children, and you kept our household running smoothly whether I was out on a flight or not. All together, we had a happy marriage for 25 years.

Epilogue

Many, many joyful times have appeared throughout my life but one of the more outstanding ones happened in 1978. It was when my wife of 6 years, Jean Clarke Russ Rust Chapman, gave me a Valentine's gift. I used that gift to register for the pilots ground school at the University of Washington in Seattle. I whipped through that fall semester of 1978 with a great deal of glee. I was a 63 year old kid!!!! It was an incredible experience to realize that soon I might be actually flying myself. I had secretly wanted to be a PAA pilot all my life. In 1939, the company wouldn't take me with glasses, even though my eyes were corrected to 20/20.

Steve Brown was a short young man, who was my class

instructor. I was happy to find out that he would be willing to give me flight instructions just as soon as the weather permitted. So when I passed all the ground school stuff, I found myself at the Boeing Flying Club, Boeing Field. We proceeded to rent a Cessna 150, checked the weather, did our preflight check and climbed aboard. I was so excited sitting in the copilots seat that I had trouble sitting still without jumping up and down. That wasn't possible as I had the seat beat fastened tightly.

When we completed our cockpit checklist, we got clearance from ground control to taxi to the active runway. Steve kept a steady patter going as to what he was doing and was expected to do. He was very detail oriented which made him a good instructor, I found. When we were finally all set we switched our communications set to the tower and got clearance to take off. That was one life experience that I have never duplicated. According to my flight log, on Feb. 3, 1979 we raced along runway 31 and ever so smoothly lifted off when the airspeed read 65 MPH. I let out an excited yell, as I found I would do on most takeoffs I would make. That moment is the MAGIC MOMENT for me, almost indescribable. I felt it back in 1939, when I took off aboard the Commodore for my first FRO training flight over Biscayne Bay. That was so many years and 10,000 flight hours ago. This emotional thrill, I've described before as an ethereal or spiritual sensation. It's just when a plane gently lifts off the runway and becomes airborne. The ground and everything you are looking down at is miniaturizing. You're climbing into a new dimension.

On May 11, 1979, I had my first solo flight in a Cessna 152. I had 17.6 hours of flight instruction and had made 32 takeoffs and landings, when Steve said "Let's go shoot some landings at Renton airport". I had just taken off from Boeing Field and was in the left hand seat. I banked to the East right over Mercer Island, where I lived, and told Renton tower we were entering the landing pattern for some touch and go's. He okayed that. I shot several touch and go's when I heard Steve ask the tower for permission to do a full stop on the taxiway. That was the first clue I had that he was about to give me my wings and let me solo. When I pulled over and stopped, he climbed out and said "Go for it Buddy. Show me what you can do with 3 t and g's. I'll be in the tower if you need me". I was so excited that I almost peed in my pants. But I felt a surge of confidence that must have been an adrenaline rush. I taxied out to the active runway and got clearance for t and g's. and the tower said okay. Then it happened.

I gave myself some flap, slowly pushed the throttle forward, kicked the rudder to keep on the centerline and got up to 65. I pulled the yolk back ever so little and smoothly lifted off the runway. I yelled loud and long. I know I must have been grin-

Only when you come close to a Boeing 747 do you get a concept of its size. This Pan Am jet was caught at San Juan International Airport, June 1971. Hal Carstens.

ning broadly as I soared up to the traffic pattern altitude of 1,200 feet. I banked left for my downwind and base legs then turned left again for my final approach and touchdown. Steve had said to do 3, but I was so incredibly excited that I disobeyed his instructions and made one more before I called the tower for permission to do a full stop and to pick up my instructor. I was so delighted to hear the tower say the words, "Congratulations Pilot, you're cleared to land." Steve said three words, when I picked him up. "Good show, Frank". Would you believe, I can see now, in my minds eye and feel the excitement of that first solo flight at Renton, Wa. 15 years ago?. Isn't memory some phenomenon, when one can do that? It gives me a pleasant shiver of excitement when I think of that solo, almost experiencing it all over again.

There were many local flights I made to such airports as Kitsap, Paine Field-Everett (where Boeing manufactures the 747's) Sheldon, Toledo, Bellevue, Anacortes, Blaine, Olympia, Ocean Shores, Chahalis and Vancouver, B.C.

Finally, I had gotten an okay from Steve to do my solo cross country. If I successfully completed that flight then I could get my official FAA private pilot's license, at long last. On a cross country, a pilot needed to plot a trip that had at least three legs of 100 miles or more on each leg. I began to very carefully plot each leg of the flight, checking weather enroute, gas needed, correct charts to cover the appropriate airports and all those details.

In the early morning of Sept 13, 1979, I took off for Portland, Oregon from Boeing Field. I was feeling great. I climbed to 8,000 feet and contacted Seattle Flight Watch, asking them for radar vectoring. That was essentially what the commercial flights do. It is also available for student pilots as well. When I checked in on VHF, I told them that I was a student pilot on my first cross country solo flight to Portland. They were very helpful and told me to set my radar identifier and squawk on a special number for me. Then they said they had me on radar and gave me my course correction to steer for Portland. It was such a comfort to know they were as close as my earphones and I couldn't stray. Half way to Portland, Seattle handed me over to Portland Flight Watch.

When I was 11 miles from Portland, Flight Watch handed me over to Hillsboro tower and I touched down nicely with a sigh of relief, I'm sure. After gassing up, I took off again for Ocean Shores. That was one of my favorite places to fly to, where you land between fairways three and four of their local golf course. The pretty ocean waves are visible only a few hundred feet away. Then I flew on to Bayview and back to Seattle, completing 5:03 minutes for the trip and totalled 53:05 flight hours.

After 121 takeoffs and landings and 69:09 hours, Steve said I was ready to take the FAA exam. I took the written and passed with no problem. But I was a bit apprehensive about the flight test.

I was scheduled for my checkout by Inspector Richard Kimball. It was a slightly gusty day but we flew anyway. It was morning of Oct. 25, 1979 when Dick said "let's go up". I'm not sure whether he felt I was going to make it or not, as it seemed he had me doing so darn many maneuvers, stalls, 360s, even a few minutes under the hood. We were flying south of Vashion Island and I was almost dizzy, when Dick said "where are we?" I looked outside and said boldly "Seattle is up there, pointing to the North and "Tacoma is there" nodding to the South. "No" he said, "Specifically where"? Frantically I scanned the chart and then looked down at the island below that we were just flying over. I grasped at straws and hoped my guess was okay, as I thought I recognized the distinctive prison we were flying over. I told him and with more relief heard him say "okay, let's go do a landing at Kitsap"

Later, I struggled to figure out the puzzle of why I didn't seem to be getting any closer to the airport. I glanced down at the ground and thought there was something really wrong. It appeared to me that we were making little or no forward speed. Thank goodness Dick finally said "we've run into strong winds that have slowed us down considerably." I just acknowledged that with a nod of my head, because I was too busy trying to get properly lined up on my downwind leg and getting ready to turn for my final approach. The wind was blowing so hard that I had to use my crabbing technique to stay lined up with the runway.

After a lucky landing and takeoff with gusty cross winds, I headed home to Boeing Field. I felt fortunate I had done so well in those windy conditions. But old stony faced Dick never said a word to me good or bad. I was still sweating profusely and worried that I hadn't done well. I landed at Boeing with no real problem and taxied to the tiedown area. As I reached up to turn the master power switch off Dick said "Okay you passed". I can tell you I was happy but too darned drained to really appreciate it. I was officially now a private pilot!. I had 76 hours in the air on Cessna-models, 150, 152, 172, 174 and 182s. Right after I had soloed, I took dear wife Jean and daughter Connie for a flight to Kitsap for lunch at the Neon Sky. Right after takeoff, I handed Jean my flight chart of the area and pointed out where we were headed and what to look for as we flew along. As we banked to the west Jean began to astound me with her comments as to exactly where we were. She'd look at the little chart in her lap then point and say oh there's the ship yard or some other somewhat obscure point we'd be flying over. I realized then that she would be a super navigator because of her fine spatial abilities. We made numerous flights together after that. One of our favorite flights was to Friday Harbor in the San Juan Islands near Bellingham, Washington. where there was a lovely picturesque restaurant overlooking the harbor. I racked up over 200 private pilot hours and it was a superior experience, worth every dollar and moment I spent in the air. Mm! Lovely memories.

Once again thanks so very much Dear Jean, for letting me do my thing and helping me get my private pilots license. My lifetime dream of being able to fly myself had at long last come true. You know how to make a guy feel ecstatic. I wish to digress one last time to describe the demise of Pan Am, to Dec. 4, 1991. Pan American World Airways had its LAST flight, when the newest of Boeing's 727, Clipper Goodwill left Bridgetowne, Barbados and headed for the city where Pan Am had started 64 years earlier, Miami. This closed a chapter in world aviation that had its meager beginning when PAAs inaugural flight took off from Key West for Havana. PAA died after a spectacular rise and explosive expansion, which regularly made history in the world of international aviation. The consensus as to why PAA collapsed seemed to be "inept management, indifferent government and extremely heavy airline competition both from domestic as well as the world"

I quote some paragraphs from the article "The Last Clipper" that Pan Am Captain Mark Pyle, the skipper of the Clipper Goodwill wrote in the Airline Pilot magazine of June 1992 about the last landing in Miami.

"As we taxied past the first formations, men and women came to a brisk attention and saluted `the last of the Clippers`. Tears welled up in my eyes then for the first time. Many rows of people and machines-all smartly formed-all saluted. I returned the salute just as crisply, fully knowing that their salutes were to this `machine` and to all the `machines` that bore the title `Clipper` for 64 years. Their salute was to the history that this ship represented and to all that had gone before."

"We passed the line of fire equipment, and the water cannon was fired over the aircraft. My emotions reeled under the weight of this tribute to Pan Am's last flight. I engaged the windshield wiper to clear the water that was on the windscreen, but that did little good for the water in my eyes. My first officer fought back his tears. He had worn Pan Am blue for 23 years."

"One final formation-all Pan American ground personnel tendered their last salute. We approached the gate and set the brakes for the last time. We shut down systems for the last time and secured the faithful engines. Sadly gathering our belongings, we shook hands. Our final flight was over. No eyes in the cockpit were dry. Many of the departing passengers shared our moment of grief. The tears will continue."

There were about 100 PAA Flight Radio Officers that I knew and can remember out of several hundred in the Communication Department. Many of the FROs I never met personally and there are a few names lost in my memory.

Jack Abernathy	E. Eckhardt	Joe Kuchta
S. Alford	Norm Ellis	Bob Laurie
Ken Barnhart	Josh Engstrom	Bill Lee
W. Bauer	Sam Everett	Larry LeKashman
Carl Berg	Peter Farrell	Charles Liese
Gus Berg	Forest Farmer	R. Mackenzie
Orville Bivens	Tom Fleming	Will March
Bjorn Bjornsen	Horatio Frazer	Pappy Martin
Ray Bourret	Ed. Fendl	Sammy Mason
Elzian Bowers	Bill Galten	Freddy Matthews
Henry Carroll	Bob Graves	G. Mayer
Herman Carroll	Fred Gussman	B. McAtee
Marty Cash	Bob Gleason	Ben McCleod
Charlie Chase*#	Orin Gould	S. Mikkleson
Ralph Conly	Dick Gebhart	W. Majewski
John Cunningham	Bob Guest	Elbridge Mills
Stan Call	Herb Hedlund	Tiny Moore
Fred Coates	Floyd Hermanson	Joe Nehring*
Fred Dixon	F. James	Bob Norloff
Spike Dawson	R. Jeffords	Henry Nicks*
Archie Deane*	Vic Johnson	D. Oliva
Pierre DeClaive	Wilson Jarboe	Oscar Olsen#
Harry Drake	Fred Kendall	Ralph Peterson
Bob Dutton	Charlie Kiernan	Pete Petragalla*
F. Dietrich	Dick Knowles	E. Pettijohn
Milt Eldred	John Krinkel	Ralph Pierson
E. Popko	Don Smith@	Jack Potter
L. Smith	Jack Poindexter	W. Sorenson
Art Prado	Butch Szabo	Paul Rafford
Tommy Temple	Harold Richardson*	Bill Todd

Ray Riley	Hubert Topliff	Al Rioux
Mike Watts	Tommy Roberts	George Whitaker
Frank Ryker	John Willmott	Dave Sanders
R. Wilson	John Sanner	J. Shattuck

#Charlie and Oscar were my Miami flight training roommates. Oscar died in China Clipper crash.

@Don was my Boston, Mass. Radio School classmate.

*I realize that I have listed a few of the highspeed CW guys at WKDL that kept Pan Am's communications world together and running smoothly for us FROs in flight and Flight Operations at Dinner Key. Thanks to all of them for that, especially those lovely young women who worked there and delivered the messages to the right places. Cities and Islands I have visited while crewing aboard Pan Am Clippers and logged over 10,000 flight hours.

Miami, Florida	San Francisco, CA
Cat Cay	Seattle, WA
Nassau, Bahamas	Ketchikan, AK
Havana, Cuba	Juneau, AK
Port au Prince, Haiti	Fairbanks, AK
Santo Domingo	Midway Isle
San Juan, PR	Wake Isle
Pointe a Petre	Guam Isle
Ffort de France	Manila, PI
Port of Spain,	Hong Kong, U. K.
Georgetown,Guy.	Bangkok, Thailand
Paramaaribo, Sur.	Suva/Nandi, Fiji
Cayenne, Guiana	Sydney, Australia
Belem, Brazil	Tokyo, Japan
Sao Luiz, Brazil	Parnamba, Brazil
Forteleza, Brazil	Natal, Brazil
Recife, Brazil	San Salvador, Brazil
Santos, Brazil	Victoria, Brazil
Rio de Janeiro, Brazil	Sao Paulo, Brazil
Lagos, Nigeria	Curityba, Brazil
Accra, Ghana	Porto Alegre, Brazil
Florianopolis, Brazil	Asuncion, Paraguay
Montivideo, Uruguay	Buenos Aires,Argentina
Barreires, Brazil	Cristobal, Panama
Kingston, Jamaica	Merida, Mexico
Camaguey, Cuba	Cienfuegos, Cuba
Johannesburg, S. A.	Leopoldville, Belgian Congo
Fisherman's Lake, Liberia	Freetown, Sierra Leone
Bathhurst, Gambia	Dakar, Senegal
Bolama, Port. Isle	Lison, Portugal
Horta/Sta Maria, Azores	Bermuda, (U. K.)
New York, N.Y.	Shediac, N. B.
Gander, Newfoundland	Shannon/Foynes, Ireland
London, U. K.	Rome, Italy
Damascus, Syria	Karachi, Pakistan
Loch Neigh, N. Ireland	Port Lyautey, Morocco

Pan Am Flying Boat Index